M000274835

AUTHOR'S NOTE

Coming to New Orleans in 1996, from Washington DC presented the usual challenges of moving and starting a new job, trying to build a house, and reading the newspaper. What was in the newspaper was stupefying; so much so that I started writing essays on the nonsense and sending them to friends. This narration goes from 1998, to the present. Some things may have changed, but not by much. Part I deals with infrastructure, ecology, the oil and gas industry, crime and corruption, and sailing. Part II is a chronology of correspondence with friends, mostly by email, of notable events in the New Orleans area. Some are absolutely hilarious and will be good conversation when you want to cheer someone up.

In dealing with crime and corruption, I am working from the principle, "If it ain't broke, don't fix it", in the opposite sense, "If it is broke, let's fix it." Nothing is going to get fixed unless it is identified and someone is willing to own it and fix it. It is being identified in a scattered and piecemeal manner through various separate investigations by local authorities and the FBI. There have been some prosecutions that punish a particular perp, but little global assessments of systems functions, and especially little effort to make this a user-friendly place for its full-time inhabitants. I do relate some admittedly simple things, especially from my personal experience, not to highlight the particular incident, but to illustrate how myriad small things that are recurrent and can't get fixed just drag a person down.

There is some racy content that has been greatly sanitized to try to avoid overtopping anyone's sensibilities. Such material has been presented in much greater detail by the media in New Orleans, and is part of the history, like it or not, not trying to avoid the obvious here. The Louisiana Office of Tourism has not offered me a job.

LiViN LAFFIN CRYiN DYiN iN COASTAL

Louisiana

HAMMOND EVE

PART I

Hammond Eve

Author has advanced degrees in wildlife biology and ecology, research experience in wildlife diseases, expertise in impacts and remediation of coal mining in Appalachia, and ecological aspects of offshore oil and gas development. Held positions as Infantry Officer, US Army; Park Ranger, National Park Service; Asst Chief of Game and Research Supervisor, OK Dept. Wildlife Conservation; Supervisory Biological Scientist, US Dept Interior; Regional Supervisor Leasing and Environment, USDI, Gulf of Mexico. He created the Appalachian Clean Streams Initiative within the USDI Office of Surface Mining. Awards include American Motors national award for exceptional service in the cause of conservation, VPOTUS Hammer Award, Bowhunting Council of Oklahoma in recognition of outstanding service to sportsmen of Oklahoma as a professional wildlife manager, Citation by special act of the legislature of the State of Oklahoma for innovative leadership, Wildlife Conservationist of the Year from the Phillips Foundation and the Oklahoma Wildlife Federation, awards for the Appalachian Clean Streams Initiative, and the Meritorious Service Award from the US Department of the Interior for Offshore management achievements. Published popular and scientific papers and speeches cover the topics of whitetailed deer disease research and management, furbearer takes, trapping and hunting, acid/toxic mine drainage prevention and management, and floating production storage and offloading platforms (ships) for offshore oil and gas operations.

INTRODUCTION

My neighbor yelled at me from across the street and asked "What brings y'all to Louisiana". Y'all in this instance would be my wife Sandra and I. He was overcome by curiosity on this issue after being over there for 15 years and just had to get it off of his chest at this point.

Providence. From the mouth of a crow. That's what, maybe.

My office in Washington DC was single occupancy first floor immediately to the right of the main entrance. This is the South Interior building, a historic building on Constitution Avenue, which overlooks the national mall. Right outside my window was a flat-topped pedestal at eye level. Someone put three pecans on top of it. A crow came along, landed on it, started trying to pick up those three pecans in his bill. This went on and on and on. I thought the crow must be utterly stupid to not understand that he could not get all of those pecans in his bill at one time. But he persisted. Eventually he got to where he had two in his bill but he could not get the third one. That got me looking carefully at the nuts at which time I realized that there were three different sizes. This crow kept on with this effort and finally got it arranged where the smallest one was at the hinge of his jaw, the next one, which would be the middle-sized, was against the smallest one and the last one was at the end of his bill. At that point he had all three of them in his bill and flew off. I thought this might be some kind of a portent, I'm not sure what kind of a portent it was. Don't give up, said the crow.

I had sent out a lot of applications, some of which I was obviously the most qualified person on earth, but got no job offers. Made me suspect that these vacancies were rigged. One day I answered the phone and Chris Oynes was on the line. He was the Regional Director of the Gulf and Atlantic regions of the Minerals Management Service. He was interested in interviewing me for the job of Regional Supervisor for Leasing and Environment. That was a stunning development. It proceeded by phone interviews, management interviews with MMS leadership in DC, and one trip to New Orleans. Things seemed to be working well.

Subsequent to the Deepwater Horizon oil spill disaster, Chris was identified worldwide as one of the 12 worst polluters according to Time Magazine, portrayed as one of the "Dirty Dozen". A picture of Chris was on the front of the magazine. More about that later. Chris spent hours on phone interviews with me. No interview I had with MMS management was adversarial; in fact, was generally pleasant. He started telling me about life in Louisiana, probably in hopes of avoiding my being shocked. His main thing one particular day was frying turkeys in people's driveways. He said come Thanksgiving everybody had their propane tank and their turkey fryer out in their driveway and they were in their Bermuda shorts and just having a grand old time and Chris got so excited about cooking and eating turkeys. This went on for a long time. I figured if I could just keep my mouth shut and listen to him talk about frying and eating these turkeys that I would probably get the job. MMS wanted a change agent, decided that I was a change agent. That stumped me, but they stuck with it.

So, Sandra and I were poised to move from Wye River in Maryland to New Orleans vicinity. At the time we had a 10,000 lb. homemade steel sailboat and trailer, a Ford pickup truck, a Mitsubishi Eclipse, and a Mitsubishi Galant. Before I even had much time to think about how difficult this might be, my Korean friend, Inhi Hong, popped up and said "you need help I go with you." I drove the truck and trailer, Sandra the sedan, Inhi the Eclipse. By the time, days later, we arrived in New Orleans (NO), we had suffered one broken axle on the trailer and four blowouts, some of which occurred in the night.

Herman Melville in the classic "Moby Dick" explained it this way: "Take almost any path you please, and ten to one it carries you down in a dale, and leaves you there by a pool in the stream. There is magic in it. Let the most absent-minded of men be plunged in his deepest reveries--stand that man on his legs, set his feet a-going, and he will infallibly lead you to water, if water there be in all that region. Should you ever be athirst in the great American desert, try this experiment, if your caravan happen to be supplied with a metaphysical professor. Yes, as everyone knows, meditation and water are wedded forever." Hence the answer to "What brought y'all to Louisiana"?

CHAPTER 1

NEW ORLEANS

New Orleans had a population of about 485,000 pre-Katrina, about 230,000 one-year post Katrina, and about 390,000 a decade post Katrina. The city merges without fanfare to the west with Metairie and Jefferson Parish. New Orleans is host to numerous huge conventions throughout the year, as well as events in the Superdome. Crime is a major concern. Many shootings, which may occur at any time and at any place, are wild acts where one or more assailants fire in the general direction of their intended targets, usually hitting several innocent people, not necessarily the intended target. Being in a crowd of people at a parade, in the middle of day, is no protection. The mindset of the typical shooting shows no plan, no consideration of an aftermath. Sometimes cameras pick up the act, more often police rely on witnesses. More criminals are caught than one would expect by these non-CSI methods.

At least seventy-one Louisiana politicians have been convicted of crimes or put on probation. From wikivisually we get this "Louisiana politicians convicted of crimes. The following 28 pages are in this category. This list may not reflect recent changes." Former Governor Edwin Edwards, former mayor Ray Nagin, and former US Representative William Jefferson are among the famous. The list missed Ronald D. Bodenheimer, a judge in Jefferson Parish, who bought a marina a stone's throw away from where I live here in Venetian Isles, within Orleans Parish. More on Ron to follow.

The oil industry headquarters have largely emigrated from New Orleans to Houston. Probable reasons for this are the difficulties in the life of this city. The public schools have been out of control, assuming the role of babysitters to hostile and undisciplined students. One of my friends who ventured into this system did not last long, asserting that the students were uncontrollable and it was hopeless to try to correct that. He left. Historically, most people with the means either lived in other communities, such as Mandeville or Covington, having to cross the longest bridge in the world twice a day, and pay a toll, or they go to local private schools, often Catholic schools.

Recent changes have the potential to improve this situation. An update is provided by Emily Langhorne (Why New Orleans Schools just made American History, Sun Herald, July, 2018). After Katrina, "The New Orleans' educational system was essentially rebuilt from the ground up as a laboratory for charter schools…an almost wholly charter-filled system largely run by the state of Louisiana. New Orleans public schools have improved faster than those of any other city in the nation over the past decade. But 80 percent of the schools were run by the state's Recovery School District. An indication of the RSD's success — and of New Orleans' resurgence as a thriving metropolitan center — is the state's decision to hand over responsibility for the school district to a locally elected school board on July 1."

The movie industry has taken a strong hold in this area. Routinely parts of the city yield to the desires of the rich and famous from Hollywood. There is a civil war era fort on the Chef Menteur Pass waterway here in my community that is used repeatedly for movies. Signs get posted all around directing movie people where to go. Innumerable trucks show up, closed trucks. They service the event, food, comfort, who knows, lots of them. There is a gun truck that produces gunfire or something like that. Sylvester Stallone has used this fort for several of his movies, as have many others. CSI New Orleans movies are made here, and occasionally one sees their activities from the highway. There is a movie studio here where inside scenes are filmed. The movie industry has free access to Fort McComb, but the public is prohibited. Probably that does not matter as Fort Pike is about 10 miles away and has public access.

Some authors have stated that the corruption is so deep in the culture here it will never be fixed. In this environment, people put up with a lot, but plenty of famous and talented people are here. Nicolas Cage had a mansion here, one among many of his assets lost to dubious financial management, as stated in the local newspaper. Ann Rice, Brad Pitt, Angelina Jolie, Jay-Z, Beyoncé, and John Goodman also have or had a residence here.

City Government and Attitudes

A useful adage at times is this, "Don't attribute to malfeasance that which can be explained by incompetence." For New Orleans, and for this state, we need a slight modification. "Don't attribute to malfeasance or incompetence that which can be explained by incompetent malfeasance".

The FBI Special Agent in Charge of the New Orleans office, Jeffrey Sallet, provided an assessment of his experience upon his departure November 3, 2017. The following is a summarization from an interview conducted by Emily Lane, NOLA.com | The Times-Picayune, on that date.

The following is Agent Sallet's commentary as reported by Ms. Lane. "I have had the unique opportunity of working in the area of corruption for the four New England states of Maine, Massachusetts, Rhode Island and New Hampshire. I had the perspective of being the national chief of corruption and civil rights, and I would say that the corruption in this state is at an extremely unacceptable level. The citizens of New Orleans and the State of Louisiana should expect and demand honest government. We have two corruption squads in the city of New Orleans. There are field offices that are five times our size that don't have that. We are very committed to eradicating it, but it's going to take a sustained effort. It's going to take commitment of the people in this state, not only the people working for the FBI, to eradicate it.

You could talk about all the nuances related to this. One is, you don't have term limits on your sheriffs and your district attorneys. Is it a healthy environment when the same family controls a parish through one of those means for decades? Do you really want to upset someone who has been in power for 30 years and may never get out of power? The way the system has been set up, there's been neglect throughout the years. The expectations of the people doing some of these jobs is, 'Hey I'm in an office, and I'm going to take what I can get.' And the people around them often fear confronting that."

"No other state has so many prominent politicians in trouble with the law. The lawbreakers are not confined to New Orleans, it is a statewide epidemic. The former Governor of Louisiana is still in jail serving a ten-year sentence; the former Elections Commissioner was convicted of crimes including money laundering; three Insurance Commissioners in a row were sent to jail; the Agriculture Commissioner has been indicted on bribery charges and the former President of the State Senate is still in jail on charges including insurance fraud and money laundering. In addition, numerous state legislators have been sent to jail on a variety of charges, including former gubernatorial candidate and KKK leader David Duke on tax fraud charges. "

"In the New Orleans area, in recent years, a very successful Wrinkled Robe investigation has netted the conviction of two Jefferson Parish judges. There has been an active investigation into the activities of the Orleans Parish School Board and several convictions have been received, including former board President Ellenese Brooks-Simms who pleaded guilty to accepting $100,000 in bribes from a consultant working for a vendor. The consultant was reported to be none other than Mose Jefferson, the brother of the indicted congressman. Another scandal involved the girlfriend of Mose Jefferson, former Councilwoman Renee Gill-Pratt, who improperly used donated vehicles that were sent to the city post-Katrina for her own personal benefit." (Jeff Crouere, Human Events, August 17, 2007)

Charity Scams

This situation is repeated time and again. In many instances it succeeds due to the absence of a whole system of government for dealing with it. There is only part of a system. This may be so because the people who ought to be ensuring an effective system are so often participants in the profits.

The process goes like this. People with political connections, usually those of long standing through generations of families following the same path, get elected. This may be to the city council, or the state legislature, or to the US Congress, or to various other elected positions. They come up with a plan for a charity, and for funding. The charity may be something specific, like to assist black male men between the ages of 16 and 25 in understanding their identity, understanding the value in honesty, work ethic, responsibility to family and employers, ethics in general, behavior, manners and speech. The mission statement may be bolstered by a definite plan, or proposal, to obtain properties in such and such areas so as to reach the most vulnerable such young men. There may be even some teaching guides. There will be a bank account to accept donations. There will be a staffing plan. It may look terrific, and if implemented it may be terrific. This is done with a sponsor in mind, or the sponsor sets it up. The sponsor is often in the state or federal legislature, with authority to introduce and promote specific spending bills. The bill may be to provide $200,000 annually to the betterment of a segment of the under-privileged black community via the Learn to Be A Man program, for trou-bled youths in New Orleans. This award will benefit the community, reduce crime, and create a chain of responsibility that will extend for generations.

The sponsor introduces the bill, it looks good, people trust it or want to do the same themselves and support it, so it passes. It is not big money in that context so it is not something to pay attention to. It passes. Implementation is to rent some rundown storefronts with an address, hire some friends and relatives to absorb the payroll, write checks to spend all the money annually with no accounting, but have 2 or 3 clients should anyone check, which is unlikely, and have an elaborate explanation as to how it will all come together next year. Money in the fraud instances will be found to be spent on clothes, jewelry, entertainment, travel, appliances, gifts. When some are found out, it is sickening as to how long it has been going on, and how obvious the lie is when it is finally examined. But the sad thing about New Orleans is that it is repeated time and again.

Red Light Cameras)

The key variable in intersections with traffic lights is the length of the yellow light warning. It should be adjusted for the speed limit of the road, longer yellow for higher speeds. In general, the yellow should last between 3 and 6 seconds. Three seconds is on the edge of being not long enough. If the yellow light is too short, the driver is trained to expect a decision crisis to drive their reaction. The crisis is caused by the short duration yellow, leading to hit the gas or hit the brakes. Neither is a safe solution. This problem is eliminated with a longer duration yellow light. Chicago is notorious for weaponizing its yellow light duration, some even getting below the sketchy 3 second minimum. (Kate Knibbs, Gizmodo, October 17, 2014)

After the citizens have been abused by an ill-conceived and malign yellow light system, in addition to becoming more hazardous drivers, they begin to hate the system, and hate the administration. The ultimate abuse of the citizen is to set up a short duration yellow light coupled with a red-light camera. The money pours into city coffers, the drivers are absolutely outraged, and often there is absolutely the nothing the citizenry can do about it, with the mayor arguing that it helps in the budget crisis. It becomes an administrative tax not approved by the voter.

If the system is not weaponized by short duration yellow lights coupled with red light cameras, it is argued that the system saves lives. The people espousing that line are the same ones benefiting from the penalties in many cases, so the exact truth of the matter may be elusive. Regardless of the exact truth, the red-light cameras are despised by most people who most often feel cheated somehow.

New Orleans has a new mayor as of this writing, LaToya Cantrell. She has made considerable improvements in community outreach and is fulfilling a campaign promise regarding red light cameras, to some extent, removing 20 from non-school related locations. Eighty will remain for school safety during school hours, and 11 will remain in high hazard areas. (Kevin Litten, NOLA. com, The Times Picayune, November 1, 2018.) A yellow light duration in the 5 second timeframe for city streets will achieve the safety desired and make the offense more digestible to the offender who is so offended.

Ex-City Councilwoman Renee Gill Pratt

A specific example of this sort of thing is seen in the activities of Renee Gill Pratt and numerous other associations of conspirators in the news of May 22, 2009. Indicted on Racketeering Charges, screams the headline from WDSU news. "A federal grand jury has indicted a former state representative and city councilwoman on racketeering charges in an alleged conspiracy involving three members of former U. S. Rep. William Jefferson's family". This was a 34-count indictment. Pratt's boyfriend, Mose Jefferson, pleaded not guilty to similar charges. Others charged were Mose's sister Betty Jefferson, and his niece Angela Coleman. They moved federal and state grant funds into other companies that they controlled and spent the money on themselves. Continuing, WDSU reported that Gill Pratt."is specifically accused of using her positions in the state Legislature and City council to use public funds for her own benefit." The accusations continue, Pratt getting $300,corrup000 in state funds for two schools when Pratt was in the Legislature, which included giving Mose a $30,000 commission from a company they controlled and somehow another $3,500 went to Pratt. She also got the city to lease space from Mose which, as this crooked wheel kept turning, resulted in Pratt getting another $5,000. Pratt was the state representative for House District 91 for 11 years and served on the City Council for 4 years. This whole mess is a convoluted web of corruption involving members of former US Congressman William Jefferson's family and friends, with tentacles in myriad directions, over time, involving a multiplicity of fake companies they controlled to confuse the money flow. This is with such hubris and involves so many people that that is in itself an indictment of the atmosphere in which the corrupted leadership of this city operates. It is a training ground for all and sundry who are seen to be following the same trend of siphoning off money through shams and spending it on themselves.

Some further legal action on the Pratt situation appeal was a bit worrisome as to justice being set back, but it turns out that the issue was not a question of guilt but a question of the sentencing guidelines. Ultimately, she was sentenced to four years in a Florida prison.

In researching the Pratt situation, which I recalled from the time, that led to more of the same as further reported by Andy Grimm of the Times Picayune. "Stacy Jackson, former head of New Orleans Affordable Homeownership, was sentenced to five years in federal prison for taking kickbacks from contractors who over-billed the non-profit agency for work rehabbing homes in poor neighborhoods that had been damaged by Hurricane Katrina. Jackson's sentence, the longest of any of the six people to face federal charges in connection with the NOAH scheme, draws a curtain on a scandal that began in former Mayor Ray Nagin's second term, when the first reports surfaced of misspending by the city's main post-Katrina blight program"

And that introduces a new group of criminals totaling six in this scheme, and so it goes, on and on, like they feed off of each other to continue the criminal activity from generation to generation, from one scheme to the other, a training ground.

It is incredible how long these charity scams have been going on, how many people have been corrupted by it, how many deserving people have been deprived by the looting. Obviously, every taxpayer charity should be audited about every six months. Top of the audit list should be any funded by state or federal line item in the budget, and especially those sponsored by any legislator, state or federal, from Louisiana.

CHAPTER 2

RAY NAGiN, MAYOR OF NEW ORLEANS, 2002-2010

Ex-Mayor Ray Nagin

C. Ray Nagin (see ray) was a Cox executive of high standing, well compensated, in a good position for life. He was sentenced to 10 years in federal prison ultimately for corrupt acts that were rather cheap in the end in comparison to his well-situated compensation at Cox. Specific charges were wire fraud, bribery and money laundering, terms that are general and vague camouflage for rampant cheating and conniving left and right.

Thinking back over the transition from his previous station in life and various notable accomplishment to politics and to jail, we see the link--New Orleans politics. He was controller at Cox, earning $400,000 annually, and part owner of the New Orleans Brass hockey team. He was an outstanding athlete and became a public figure through hosting a twice weekly television show. As William Jefferson in the end ruined many people, so too did Ray Nagin. The crusading Times Picayune gave us daily fare on this. Part of the daily fare was Ray's sticky fingers in the public till, in high end New Orleans restaurants, with his wife Seletha, another victim of his criminality. Assured by arrogance, eating high on the hog, in public view, repeatedly, and charging it to the city, he explained that it was city business, as he and his wife chowed down, since everywhere he went someone asked him some question about some city enterprise, or made some comment related to New Orleans, therefore it became a business meal, and he used his city credit card to pay for it, and thought there would never be a reckoning.

His blindness to how offensive this was to the public, regardless of how many times he got called on it, typifies a loss of contact with reality and a loss of appreciation of justice. From a small beginning a river of corruption flowed. This reminds me of the outrage, going uncorrected, where city employees in city vehicles would take long midday lunch and shopping sprees parking in no parking zones on Magazine street, privileged and arrogant, knowing they could get away with it and not caring about damage to public trust.

Home Depot Gets Down Home Treatment

Home Depot wanted to put a store in central New Orleans which would consume several blocks of existing development, thus requiring some sort of condemnation. To demonstrate the effect of New Orleans reputation for corruption in the larger context of this country, the executives at Home Depot, when confronted with Ray's proposition, naturally assumed it was business as usual. For the city to proceed with clearing this land of inhabitants and buildings and enterprises, and removing and rerouting streets that impinged, Ray proposed that Home Depot would become sponsor of a countertop maker and installer to be called Stone Age. This would be a new business enterprise for him and his sons. There is lots of fodder on where the materials for this countertop business came from that were questionable, thus expanding the multiplicity of things to be investigated. Also, was Home Depot in trouble over this? Was it some sort of bribery, or business as usual? How difficult this gets to be, how ensnaring it is to people who had no intention of doing wrong.be touched by this city government.

Juliet Linderman, (NOLA.com, the Times Picayune,) put it this way " "Prosecutors in the Ray Nagin corruption trial on Tuesday began calling witnesses to back up charges that the former New Orleans mayor in 2007 used his political influence to help kill a community benefits agreement connected to construction of the Home Depot store in Central City while actively soliciting contracts from the big box retailer for his family's granite counter-top business, Stone Age LLC. Sarah Price, former senior manager at Home Depot, reviewed for the jury a series of internal emails in which she expressed concern that about the mayor's interest in pursuing contracts. The first internal email shown to the jury from a Home Depot official, dated Dec. 27, 2006, mentioned that Nagin left a voice mail for Home Depot's southern division head asking to discuss potential bids for Stone Age. In response, Home Depot senior manager Eric Criss wrote, "These guys better be damned careful. Didn't we just get an incentive from New Orleans?" Price testified that indeed, Home Depot had received an incentive from the city. In her email response, Price wrote that it was "dangerous to use an elected official family business. "But at the time Home Depot was also negotiating a community benefits agreement championed by Councilwoman Stacy Head, that would have required the store to employ neighborhood residents at above-market rates and offer them health benefits and a 401k retirement plan. According to Price, "there was a lot of back and forth" about the agreement, which Home Depot was never inclined to support. Price testified that on Jan. 29, 2007, she received an email saying that Nagin had called "to offer Home Depot his full support." Price told the jury that hours later, she sent a fax to Head, discontinuing the community benefits agreement." All this string pulling by a host of characters puts the nefarious and the innocent into the same mix of possible jeopardy with the law.

The FBI was probing questionable city contracts and contractors related to data management and crime cameras, thinking that Nagin was "more of a bumbler than a crook" This notion was squelched when Newark NJ business-man Michael McGrath, who was implicated there in a $136 million mort-gage fraud scheme, casually mentioned that he was instrumental in getting a $50,000 bribe to the Mayor of New Orleans.

This brings up a whole new host of characters that are now jailed, the New Orleans technology chief Greg Meffert and city vendor Mark St. Pierre. Greg's wife, Linda, was implicated, but as this played out, in consideration of the couple's two children, a bargain was reached where Greg would be imprisoned for the crimes and Linda would be spared to support the children.

This story spreads out from here like legs, or is it arms, on an octopus. Every leg has a sucker with teeth. Starting with Nagin, someone took him and his family on a Hawaiian vacation. That someone is New Orleans Technology Chief Greg Merrett, and New Orleans City Vendor [contractor] Mark St. Pierre, or some combination thereof. Whether Nagin knew who was picking up the tab is not known, but what is known is that it was not Nagin. Since Meffert and St. Pierre at one time were a package, separated in name only by the roles they came to play in the New Orleans saga of wide corruption under Nagin, this vacation could hardly have been shrouded in secrecy as to how it was financed. Other such trips by Nagin backers took him to Jamaica and Chicago.

Meffert, St. Pierre, and Other Legs of the Octopus

The leg with Meffert and others regarding the crime cameras involved Dell, Inc, the computer maker, Southern Electronics and Active Solutions, crime camera technology specialists, and Veracent, a St. Pierre firm, and possibly Netmethods, due to the fact that one person represented both Veracent and Netmethods. From here the adage that comes to mind is "round and round it goes, where it stops nobody knows". Somewhere in the ensuing mess the proposed camera supplier, Dell, ran afoul of a 15-state prohibition on sale of cameras to those states, not sure of exactly how that was worded. This led to highly intelligent people looking for a way around that stricture and came up with new names for cameras, calling them "eyeballs" and "surveillance modules". Louisiana apparently was party to the 15-state prohibition, so sales proceeded in the aftermath of Katrina nonetheless in various cities in Louisiana.

The state purchasing agency froze all these contracts in March 2007, leading to various legal actions.

The outcome of this mess has been nicely documented as follows by Brendan McCarthy and Eliot Kamenitz {The Times Picayune, October 5, 2009}: "More than 250 crime cameras have been installed in New Orleans, but only about 85 are operable. Days before thousands of citizens marched on City Hall last year in a public outcry about crime, Mayor Ray Nagin held a twilight news conference to outline crime-fighting initiatives. One key to the plan: The mayor championed crime surveillance cameras as an unassailable witness to help take back the city's neighborhoods. On that January evening in 2007, Nagin announced that 50 cameras would be operable within a week, with 200 online by the end of the year. It was a modest proposal, scaled down from an earlier pledge of 1,000 cameras. Even the more modest goal remains elusive. Since the announcement, much of the Nagin administration's crime camera program has been cloaked in secrecy. City Council members and citizens seeking basic information about the program, such as contracts, have been rebuffed. As a City Council hearing about the matter began Tuesday morning, the city's technology officer, who is in charge of camera deployment, was nowhere to be found. A note sent to the head of the Public Works committee stated that Anthony Jones -- who had canceled several previously scheduled appearances -- was traveling. That left two attendees, a police officer and an associate tasked with monitoring the program, to give council members the bad news: Right now, the city has "about 85 cameras that work most of the time."

On a small and personal scale which illustrates the stupid and blind self-serving actions of Nagin, we have this. Katrina blew the shingles off the roofs of thousands of houses along the gulf coast, leaving exposed wood that would leak rainwater down through the house, with major damage to ceilings, walls, furniture, belongings. Common sense and the insurance companies wanted this quickly covered, even if temporary to contain the damages and costs. A federal agency, probably FEMA, came up with the blue tarp program to nail

15

these tarps free of charge to houses so damaged. In New Orleans, the administrators of this program developed a signup plan, first come first served, for the New Orleans area. At this time, utilities were absent or scant, supplies of all types lacking, roads and bridges damaged, transportation curtailed. To get signed up, a person had to go to New Orleans to the facility designated, wait in line for hours, and get signed on. This worked as expected till Nagin decided to intervene. He decreed the first come first serve approach would be abandoned because he wanted an even blue wave to emanate from a center and spread evenly outward, so as to avoid a splotchy appearance from the air. That killed the program for those not close to the center of the city, for me and my neighbors.

No graft was too small for Nagin. His lawn service, which was $200 per month, was paid for by Jimmy Goodson through a company Goodson owned. Goodson was an associate of Mark St. Pierre, who was a city vendor. City vendor means city contractor. This was at St. Pierre's instigation.

Several days prior to leaving office at the end of his second term, Nagin said "there was no corruption under my watch.

CHAPTER 3

THE FEDERAL BUREAU OF INVESTiGATiON (FBI)

The FBI, headquartered in Washington, DC, has 56 Field Offices located in major cities and about 400 resident agencies in smaller cities. Each Field Office is headed by a Special Agent in Charge. As of 2006, there were about 30,000 employees comprised of about 12,500 agents and about 17,500 support personnel. The New Orleans office covers the state and has about 400 employees.

As is apparent from this catalog of crimes and prosecutions, the FBI in New Orleans is an essential counterweight to corruption, employing investigative tools that are cutting edge, using cooperators effectively to nail the crooks with indisputable evidence, and developing effective prosecution strategies for their court actions. Two major cases are relevant in this narration to portray the criminal environment in south Louisiana. The first is Operation Wrinkled Robe; the second is the waste disposal situation. The first is typical of the FBI's effective investigative and prosecutorial capabilities, but the second went astray through the careless and mindless ego-driven actions of two agents who effectively but unintentionally sabotaged the prosecution. Even though final prosecution in the waste management situation has not and may never be consummated, the information arising from the FBI investigation should be a warning to anyone in government working in the waste management arena as to how elements may be manipulated.

Operation Wrinkled Robe was the FBI designation for its investigation into various elements and personnel in the court systems in this area. The many successful prosecutions of the various judges and others of the court were often outcomes from this investigation and will not be repeated in this section.

Jim Ward and Fred Heebe owned the River Birch landfill which was situated near the Jefferson Parish landfill. The two landfill owners were suspected of persuading officials of Aaron Broussard's administration to close down the Jefferson Parish landfill and send the garbage to the River Birch landfill. This had the potential to enrich Jim and Fred, but it ran afoul of the FBI investigation. A technical side issue came into play early on, and that was the solidification of odiferous liquid waste, which River Birch was not equipped to handle. Aside from the investigation of the matter and the court proceedings, a most interesting development materialized in the public media.

The most interesting and surprising part of this saga was the actions of two FBI agents playing the media reporting. Sal Perricone was the federal prosecutor in the case, and as proceedings were publicized, especially in the newspaper, Sal entered commentary about his own performance in court under the guise of two anonymous pen names, congratulating himself in writing, as if he were an astute member of the public. One other agent was involved in this. Fred Heebe and possibly others saw a similarity in the wording Periconne used in court with the wording some commenters used in the newspaper and began to wonder if Periconne were playing the media, the public and his agency with his commentary about himself. Hebee hired a text analyzer, former FBI agent, to pursue this. Outcome was that Perricone was outed as one of the commenters. Hebee then presented the argument that the trial was bent by Perricone actions to commend himself and should then be thrown out of court or something like that. The trial was abandoned in some fashion after this and Jim Letten, the Special Agent in Charge, was an unfortunate victim of this shenanigan, some said due to his trusting his agents too much. This waste management narration is supported by Chad Chandlers piece in The New Orleans Advocate, August 20, 2018, and my memory of the situation from that time;

CHAPTER 4

EX-JUDGE R. BODENHEIMER

"The FBI's nine-year inquiry into Courthouse corruption and the ensuing prosecutions convicted 14 people of federal crimes, imprisoned two judges and removed a third from office through impeachment. And it grew out of a simple tip that the Metropolitan Crime Commission received on June 15, 1998, according to FBI records". .."newly released FBI records of its investigation, which sent district judges Ronald Bodenheimer and Alan Green to prison, obtained guilty pleas from 12 others, including Sheriff's Office jailers, and culminated last December with the Senate kicking U.S. District Judge Thomas Porteous out of office." (Drew Broach, NOLA.com, The Times Picayune, January 12, 2018}

Judge Ronald Bodenheimer is close to this neighborhood, Venetian Isles, as his ambitions, trampling law and covenants, led to killing one young man and injuring another about 400 yards from my back deck. Ron was the judge handling a divorce settlement between a successful restauranteur and his wife. At issue was who would get custody of their son, as both vied for it. The restaurant chain owned by the father of the couple was big into seafood dishes and consequently bought tons of shrimp on a regular basis. Ron wanted in on what he perceived as a gravy train, becoming a shrimp supplier for the restaurant chain. A marina had been situated in Venetian Isles, but had been wiped out by Katrina. Covenants related to the property were such that if the marina failed, no new marina and owner would be allowed to resume the business, it would revert to residential rather than commercial property. Ron acquired the property nonetheless, somehow, and proceeded to build up the marina.

Next, he had to get a supply of shrimp coming in, in large measure, through his marina and into the restaurant chain, to fulfill his ambitions. On the shrimp side, he had a conveyor built to get the shrimp from the coolers on the shrimp boats into the refrigerated storage of the marina. Without submitting plans to the city, or submitting flawed plans, he scrabbled together a make-shift apparatus, powered by shore power electricity, this was not inspected or approved by the city. Early in its use, a couple of young fellows showed up with their shrimp boat and started loading up the conveyor and powered it on. One was man was electrocuted, the other knocked into the water.

The other prong to Ron's scheme was to get a contract with the restaurant chain to sell his shrimp. Since he was judge in the custody case with the owner of the restaurant chain, he started conniving to convey custody to the dad if the chain would commit to buying his shrimp.

A neighborhood detractor and vocal critic of the marina operation generated Ron's ire. Ron said, he just does not know who he is dealing with. Ron had a drug dealer plant OxyContin in the glove compartment of this fellow's car and sicced the cops on the critic. Ron was caught in his own snare.

"

These events were publicized by The Advocate as follows: "The unfolding saga of Jefferson Parish Judge Ronald Bodenheimer is straight out of a bad TV movie. The nutshell version: Bodenheimer owned an eastern New Orleans marina targeted by complaints of drug activity and zoning violations. The criticism grew after a teenager died in an electrocution accident on a marina conveyer belt earlier this year. Bodenheimer's response to the loudest marina critic, according to the FBI, was to try and shut him up by conspiring to plant illegal drugs in his vehicle. The FBI, which said it uncovered all this during a sweeping courthouse corruption probe, charged Bodenheimer with criminal conspiracy and drug violations. His trial is set for March. Federal prosecutors hope to get the cooperation of a witness who may testify about Bodenheimer's alleged involvement in a Metairie drug-smuggling ring. Jefferson Parish President Tim Coulon also admitted he met privately with Bodenheimer in April to ask for a lenient sentence for his brother-in-law, who had been convicted in Bodenheimer's court of molesting teenage girls. Just when you thought it couldn't get any sleazier, accusations surfaced that Bodenheimer, presiding over restaurant magnate Al Copeland's child-custody case, awarded Copeland generous benefits in the hope that Copeland would respond with an offer to grant lucrative seafood contracts to Bodenheimer. The embattled judge remains suspended with pay." (Gambit, December 30, 2002)

CHAPTER 5

EX-JUDGE ALAN GREEN

"**Y**ou have to give political money to the court, to all the judges. I'm talking about thousands, not hundreds." (Lori Marcotte, Former Vice President and CEO Bail Bonds Unlimited, Tulanelink.com)

Michelle Kruupa, (Tulanelink.com, June 23, 2005) reports as follows:

"To the top executives of Bail Bonds Unlimited, Judge Alan Green was different from his colleagues on the 24th Judicial District Court bench. "He asked for cash, and he put it in his pocket," Lori Marcotte, the company's former vice president and chief executive officer, told jurors Wednesday during Green's corruption trial. Tearing to the core of the federal government's case, Marcotte, who is the sister of Louis Marcotte III, the admitted ringleader of the Jefferson Parish Courthouse racket, characterized one of the dozens of payments that prosecutors allege Bail Bonds Unlimited employees gave Green to entice him to set bonds for criminal defendants so the firm could turn a profit. "It was a bribe. It was like our little secret," said Lori Marcotte, who along with her brother has pleaded guilty to a felony in the Operation Wrinkled Robe investigation. Louis Marcotte also is a potential government witness."

Marcotte explained that Judges Green and Bodenheimer were in her office every day, the go-to judges.

Green was sentenced to 51 months in prison

CHAPTER 6

EX-US REP WiLLiAM JEFFERSON AND BETTY

"**O**h, what a tangled web we weave, when first we practice to deceive!" (Sir Walter Scott, 1808)

William Jennings Jefferson (Bill, Dollar Bill) was born March 14, 1947 on a farm in Lake Providence, East Carroll parish, in NE Louisiana. He had eight siblings. Bill and his wife Angela have five daughters, all well-educated. Bill earned a law degree from Harvard Law in 1972 and a degree in taxation from Georgetown Law in 1996. He was a Louisiana State Senator for the 5th district from 1980 to 1991, then served Louisiana 2nd District in the US House of Representatives from 1991 to 2009.

Bill's earliest known duplicity came to light when a tech company named iGate paid him $400,000 through a company owned by his family members. The purpose of this payoff was to get Bill to persuade the US Army to test iGate's technology products and to persuade the governments of Nigeria, Ghana, and Cameroon to engage in a business deal with iGate pursuant to financing by the Export-Import Bank of the United States.

A woman named Lori Mody had a company and interest in the development of a broadband infrastructure in Nigeria. She became a cooperator with the

27

FBI and wore a wire in a meeting with Bill at which time Bill informed her that the Nigerian Vice President required $500,000 to ensure that iGate and Mody's company obtained the contracts for broadband service in Nigeria. Bill said he would give the money to the VP. This led to the world-famous seizure of $90,000 from Bill's freezer pursuant to a legal search warrant. The money was part of a $100,000 cash payoff made by Modi and videotaped by the FBI. The serial numbers in the freezer cache were the same as those given to Modi by the FBI to give to Bill.

Bill wanted a percentage of any broadband deals in Nigeria that were consummated in income for the companies he had tentacles in, arranging for his family to have a 5 to 7 percent ownership stake in the Nigerian internet company. He sought $10,000,000 from Modi for services to be rendered in regard to his anticipated involvement in whatever developed. The FBI asserted that they had "at least seven other schemes in which Jefferson sought things of value in return for his official acts.

Jefferson was indicted on 16 charges of corruption by a federal grand jury, pled not guilty, in June, 2007. About two years later, after much back and forth with the courts, he was convicted on 11 of the 16 corruption charges. He was sentenced to 13 years in prison. About three years after that, the U.S. Court of Appeals upheld the conviction on ten of the eleven charges. In 2017, pursuant to other changes in the basis of law for this situation, seven charges were dropped and Bill's sentence was reduced to time served, which was 5 years five months. This may be revisited in the future pending other legal outcomes for some elements of this case that have yet to be resolved. (The information in this narrative on William Jefferson has been derived from many reports in the Times Picayune, Wikipedia, and an FBI report)

Barbara Jefferson Jackson, known as Betty Jefferson in many venues, older sister to former US Representative William Jefferson, was born in 1938, and elected to two terms (2002 and 2006) as New Orleans Assessor for the Forth Municipal District. She died in 2013.

In general, she had access to several taxpayer funded charities' funds and the bank accounts of the assessor's office. She pleaded guilty to looting these funds. Looking for the specifics of these charges we have the report of Gordon Russell, NOLA.com, The Times Picayune, on possible misappropriations. There is $114,000 from Jefferson's work account,11 checks from her assessor's account to "straw payees" and cashing the checks herself, 79 expenditures totaling $50,725 without providing any supporting documentation, $22,000 to Jefferson or members of her family, 80 checks to herself totaling $57,623, 9 checks to "cash" totaling $5,448. At least five checks were made out to an office employee, Tammi Tucker, but were cashed by a member of Jefferson's family, who forged Tucker's name and kept the money, the audit says Auditors also couldn't determine whether any of the checks were written for a legitimate business purpose because Jefferson kept no documentation

She pled guilty in 2010 and got 5 years' probation and 15 months of home detention. As I recall, the reason for this lenient sentence was that her daughter was in severe ill health and could not manage without care and that care reasonably should come from her mother.

Ms. Jefferson had served a sentence of 15 months home detention after admitting to her hand in a scheme to pilfer more than $1 million in public funds through several phony charities her family controlled. "I wish I could explain it. It was awful," Ms. Jefferson said of her deeds during her testimony. "I'd say it's the sinful nature. Whatever happened got started and kept going. I cannot point to it, I don't know, but it was a sinful act." (Richard Rainey, Politics, nola.com, 2013}

CHAPTER 7

CiTY SANiTATiON
FEE DEBACLE

"The past sanitation-fee scofflaws even included Cynthia Hedge-Morrell, a city councilwoman at the time, and her husband, Clerk of Criminal District Court Arthur Morrell."(Charles Maldonado, The Lens, The New Orleans Advocate, April 20, 2015). This is the story of how an informed elite can get garbage pickup without paying for it due to flaws in the collection and enforcement provisions regarding trash fees appended to the water bill. The Sewerage and Water Board (SWB) historically had enforcement authority over the city water supply and billing, and an administrative capability regarding processing bills and payments. The trash administrative element did not have a billing and collection capability nor a penalty capability.

The New Orleans solution to this system, instead of making it a robust and defensible public service, decided to simply append the trash fee to the water bill without any ability to collect and enforce the payment. Trying to make this sideways scheme acceptable to the public, they played the humanitarian card and said the last thing any human being would want to do would be to cut off a person's water supply. Even passed a law that if a person paid for the water part, the city was prohibited from cutting off the water if they did not pay for the trash part.

31

For those folks who are honest, or ignorant of this glitch, it was a bill to be paid in full, the total indicated on the bill. For those who are apprised with inside knowledge of the city's inability to enforce the payment of the trash fees, it was a prime opportunity to cheat. This is not something that can be overlooked. Every month a bill comes in, with both charges presented. Every person who failed to pay their full share, every month chose to steal from those who did, for their trash got collected, but someone else paid for it. Every month. When this matter with the Morrells became exposed, the did explain. Arthur paid the bills and Cynthia just did not know anything at all about it. Plenty of people were in on this, and there have been and are efforts to fix it, but that's not saying much since things here can be fixing to get fixed for decades. Here is a bothersome element to this story.

Commissioned by the Greater New Orleans and Ford foundations, the Assets and Opportunities Profile found that the poverty rate in the Crescent City is 27 percent, compared to a national average of 15 percent, and that 37 percent of all New Orleans residents are afflicted by asset poverty (philanthropynews-digest.org). We can rest assured that those in need, the 37 percent, for the most part will be paying their bills in total. The city is in budget crisis perpetually. The insiders and the scofflaws, wherever they are and whoever they may be, need to be brought into the corral, so the destitute don't wind up supporting the affluent, which is the existing situation.

According to a 2013 audit by the New Orleans Inspector General's Office, the deficit arising from this situation amounted to $8.5 million in 2011. Bruce Egger, (NOLA.com, September 14, 2011), presents some interesting information on this. The New Orleans Department of Finance lists 611 customers with outstanding sanitation bills exceeding $2000. Incredibly, one such customer owes $74,896.

Getting back to the Morrells and how it turned out, we have this from Gordon Russell, (NOLA.com, the Times Picayune, August 25, 2011). " One of New Orleans' leading political couples went nearly a decade without paying their sanitation bill until a local television station questioned them about it this week. WVUE-TV reported Wednesday that the trash bill for the Gentilly home owned by Clerk of Criminal Court Arthur Morrell and his wife, New Orleans City Councilwoman Cynthia Hedge-Morrell, had reached $2,648 by June. The Sewerage & Water Board, which bills for sanitation fees, could not provide the Morrells' records to The Times-Picayune on Thursday. But Hedge-Morrell did not deny the television report, issuing a statement late Wednesday saying that she had settled the outstanding bill. She said that her husband, a lawyer, had decided not to pay the bills because he had "constitutional concerns" about them. In an interview Thursday with the newspaper, Arthur Morrell said he wasn't positive about what sparked his refusal to pay the sanitation fee. His concerns weren't precisely constitutional, he said, but he "had a problem with a public agency collecting for a private company." Private company or not, he used the service and knew someone else was paying for his use of it. For nearly 10 years.

Where is the blame. Relatively speaking, this geographic area is an ethics black hole with regard to elected and appointed officials. Ethical considerations will not solve this deficiency and it clearly will not solve itself. Is the legislature lazy? There must be a secret cabal that is effective at maintaining the status quo. Someone is benefiting from it. This is the latest I could find about it. "No New Orleans home or business has been cut off from city water service for failure to pay trash fees, despite the passage more than a year ago of a city ordinance that granted such punitive power to Mayor Mitch Landrieu's administration." Separate it from any connection to city water and provide an enforcement tool for trash. If they don't pay, don't pick it up and get them with something like blighted property regulations. A paper route provides papers to subscribers and not all people subscribe. It would be annoying for the garbage guys to have to keep track of who is paying. Work it out. Save millions.

CHAPTER 8

WHERE THE HELL iS SLiDELL

So said the custom T shirts some government employees in DC started wearing upon notice that they were Slidell bound. Everybody around here knows where it is. You go east over the high rise and cross the twin span and you are there, unless you take a bender to the left at Irish Bayou and rattle your way across the 5 mile bridge.

I thought the concept of corruption down here was sufficiently noted by the mostly New Orleans situation, but the Slidell notables do have a strong entry. Former St. Tammany Parish District Attorney Walter Reed served as district attorney for 30 years for St. Tammany and Washington Parishes. He was convicted on corruption charges about 3 years ago. On April 1, he begins serving a 4-year prison sentence for mail fraud, wire fraud, income tax evasion, and other charges. (Former DA must report to prison April 1. Robert Roden, The Times Picayune, February 27, 2019). Those are perfectly uninformative characterizations of criminal acts.

In the article "Former St. Tammany Parish District Attorney Walter Reed faces state ethics charge", (theadvocate.com JUL 28, 2015) Sara Pagones, adds some flesh to that skeletal outline. Reed received $82,500 from the St. Tammany Parish Hospital that he deposited in his personal bank account during the period Aug. 4, 2011, to March 27, 2014. Those by law were "funds due his public agency," not due to him personally. He actually got more that,

35

$572,067, but the statute of limitations prevented his being charged for all of it. Prior to that, over a span of about 5 years, he took $30,000 a year from he hospital for fees that should have gone to his office.

If he were found guilty on all 18 counts in a federal indictment, he would face 277 years in prison. This last projection reminds one of ex-governor Edwin Edwards, who famously said, while standing on the courthouse steps facing similar sentencing, something like, "if convicted on all charges I will not serve out those sentences".

Concerning the federal charges, Katie Moore provides the outcome. (4WWL News, November 5, 2018) in the following article:" Federal appeals court upholds former DA Walter Reed's corruption conviction" "The U.S. Court of Appeal for the Fifth Circuit upheld Reed's 2016 conviction on 18 corruption and fraud charges Monday afternoon…ranging from conspiracy to fraud for, among other things, using campaign contributions for personal use. They found his son Steven Reed guilty on three counts." Once again, the father makes a convicted criminal of his son.

The other notable is former St. Tammany Parish coroner Dr Peter Galvan. Galvan "was sentenced to serve 24 months in federal custody followed by one year of supervised release, fined $5,000, and ordered to pay restitution of at least $193,388. Galvan pled guilty to conspiring to steal government funds from the St. Tammany Parish Coroner's Office. (Department of Justice. U.S. Attorney's Office, Eastern District of Louisiana, February 12, 2014)

Further details from that DOJ document show that Galvan took unearned sick leave and got paid for it in the amount of $111,376 over a 5 year period. Galvan entered into a personal contract to provide medical services for the jail, but assigned one of his employees from his coroner's office to fulfill the contract. Galvan used at least $50,000 in public funds to pay the other employee to fulfill his (Galvan's) contract. Apparently, the jail paid Galvan for work the coroner's office employee did.

"Additionally, Galvan conspired with an employee of the coroner's office to purchase a $9,170 generator for Galvan's personal vessel, a life raft and life jackets for his personal vessel valued at $4,841, and a Global Positioning Satellite Receiver for his personal use valued at $2,395, all with St. Tammany Parish Coroner's Office funds. Finally, Galvan used his St. Tammany Parish Coroner's Office credit card to make purchases of meals and other personal items with his public credit card totaling $15,606 which were unrelated to the office's business" (Department of Justice, February 12, 2014.

U.S. Attorney Kenneth Allen Polite, Jr. stated that residents of this state are tired of corruption.

Jack Strain was sheriff of St. Tammany Parish for 20 years, ending in 2016. Two deputies under Strain set up a company, Workforce Solutions, ostensibly owned by the deputies' children, to operate an inmate release program. The two deputies pled guilty to "profiting from a Department contract while maintaining their public employment in a scheme the federal government says involved former Sheriff Jack Strain". The Bill of Information states that Strain set up no bid contracts to award the job to Workforce Solutions. The children received about $1,200,000 through this scheme. The money was distributed upward through the participants. In exchange for this noncompetitive award to his deputies' children, Strain received $1000 on a recurring basis over a 4-year period. The Workforce Solutions investigation led to a separate probe of allegations that Strain sexually abused 4 to 5 teenagers., dating back to before Strain became sheriff in 1996. Strain has not been charged with a crime. (Robert Roden, Former deputies plead guilty to fraud, bribery. The Times Picayune. March 1, 2019.

CHAPTER 9

MISSISSIPPI RIVER

The Mississippi River flows about 2350 miles from Lake Itasca, Minnesota, to the Gulf. It provides drinking water for about 18 million people in 50 states. There are 29 lakes and dams. It handles about 60 per cent of the grain that is exported from the United States and billions of dollars in freight. Sometimes it is referred to erroneously as "The Big Muddy", but much of that mud comes from the real "Big Muddy", which is in Southern Illinois, flowing into the Mississippi

The river was discovered by Hernando deSoto just below Natchez in 1541. There were many exploratory efforts to find the mouth from Gulf, but there were several factors that made this difficult. There are three main passes from the gulf to the head of the river, termed the birds foot, and several smaller ones. The Head of Passes is where these passes join. This is considered the mouth of the Mississippi, and it is inland from the gulf shoreline. Dating back centuries, entry into the river was a problem due to several passes from the Gulf, making it confusing. Also, longitude could not be calculated until the mid-1700's due to timepieces of inadequate accuracy for navigational calculations. This meant that no one could determine exactly where they were along the gulf coast, nor could they later return to an exact location along the coastline. Commerce would be delayed until this problem got solved.

If you visit the French Quarter and stand on the river bank and look across, and you have some sort of a sense of direction, and you thought this river flowed South, and you observe that it is flowing North, and you think Alzheimer's has finally set in, don't worry. It is flowing North, at that point. That is, after it has flowed East from Baton Rouge. To make sure visitors stay confused, natives refer to the East Bank and the West Bank. If you happen to be in Memphis, this makes sense cause the East bank is on the East side etc. But that nomenclature carries all the way to the Gulf. So, in your position on the bank there in the French Quarter, not only is the river flowing North, but you are standing on the East bank despite the fact that you are on the West side of the river, and as you gaze East at the other bank, that is the bank that is east of you, that would be the West bank.

The river, as with other sediment laden rivers, dams itself at the outfall downstream. Flowing swiftly and deep and loaded with sediment, the sands and mud are carried downstream until the flow rate decreases, at which time the entrained sands settle to the bottom where the Mississippi River meets the Gulf of Mexico. The main agent to get this done is the river's widening and becoming shallow at the mouth. Eventually, over the centuries, this builds up to the point that the flow, especially during flood events, backs up, causing the river to break out of its banks upstream and cut a new channel.

The shipping channel is used by over 6,000 cargo ships every year, averaging 16 per day, that export grain around the world, produced by farmers up and down the river. It is often clogged with mud and silt. The solution is dredging that shipping channel.'(Paul Aucoin and Sean Duffy. The Maritime Executive. March 2, 2017.)

The US Army Corps of Engineers has built levees on both sides of the river for hundreds of miles. These levees have constrained the rechanneling aspect and led to people's getting established in hazardous areas should the levee overtop. Historically, before the levees, this breaking out served to renew the land and keep back the salt water where it belongs. As settlers depended on the levees to curtail the river, they moved into previous flood zones that will again turn into a flood zone with a levee break, leading to loss of life, property and sustenance. The oystermen working in the coastal marshes depend on the salt water to keep the oysters healthy. With a levee overtopping, previously healthy beds become oyster cemeteries.

In the last century, some adventurous, or crazy, people became squatters on the lands between the bank of the river and the levee. This is pretty much going to flood sooner or later, but they chose to live there, eating most everything that walks, crawls, swims or flies. Early commerce on the river involved building huge wooden rafts far upstream, loading them with sale goods, and going city to city doing deals till they wound up around New Orleans, where they would dismantle the rafts and sell the wood.

Along the coast, the marshes sink due to natural subsidence. The oil companies cut many canals for access and pipelines. These two factors, and natural erosion have led to a retreating coastline. This caused the sediment accumulations, over the millennia, to become isolated islands, curving to match the depositional pattern from the damming phenomenon. This can be seen on a state road map that shows the Chandeleur Islands out from Gulfport, Mississippi.

The oceanic flow enters the Gulf between Cuba and Yucatan, heading North toward New Orleans. It branches, one arm going west to die in eddies off Mexico. The other goes East and carries sediments and detritus from the river to be deposited on the beaches just to the East, somewhat into Mississippi.

Portions of the river are hazardous due to e. coli bacteria from human and animal waste. Some stretches have too much phosphorus which is harmful in excess because it promotes algal growth which depletes oxygen levels, kills fish, and coats the seafloor, inhibiting animal life when it dies and settles to the bottom. (State of the River Report, 2016, www.stateoftheriver.com)

Just because the river is caffeinated does not mean you should change your morning coffee routine. It's not that strong. Besides the caffeine, there are eleven other chemical contaminants in the river, at least. (Contaminants in the Mississippi River. U.S. GEOLOGICAL SURVEY CIRCULAR 1133, Reston, Virginia, 1995, Edited by Robert H. Meade.)

The caffeine comes from leaky septic systems throughout the watershed. The other contaminants, in part, come from runoff of non-point sources. This means there is no discrete flow, but surface runoff that follows the contours and exits in sheet flow or seeps or trickles over numerous drains.

These contaminants find their way to the Gulf and create the Dead Zone. The dead zone is a large ecological disaster out from the mouth of the river, caused by outflow contaminants from the river, that attracts much interest, concern, and anxiety as to what to do about it. The usual outcome of this emotion is a throwing up of the hands in defeat. It's just too big to manage. The solution would require government intrusion into management of thousands of agricultural operations and that would be politically untenable. If we want a government project that would be helpful, taking this on would be less of a project than putting levees along both sides of the river for thousands of miles, less than putting a rock apron along a thousand miles of shoreline.

Surface mining operations face the same issues that a farm does in terms of runoff. A surface mine is required to manage drainage to achieve control. This leads to channeling the drainage into sediment ponds where it is treated if necessary, sediments settle out, and the drainage becomes a point source that is checked periodically to ensure that the outflow is harmless.

The Dead Zone

"Dead zones are hypoxic (low-oxygen) areas in the world's oceans and large lakes, caused by "excessive nutrient pollution from human activities coupled with other factors that deplete the oxygen required to support most marine life in bottom and near-bottom water. This large dead zone size shows that nutrient pollution, primarily from agriculture and developed land runoff in the Mississippi River watershed is continuing to affect the nation's coastal resources and habitats in the Gulf. These nutrients stimulate massive algal growth that eventually decomposes, which uses up the oxygen needed to support life in the Gulf. This loss of oxygen can cause the loss of fish habitat or force them to move to other areas to survive, decreased reproductive capabilities in species and a reduction in the average size of shrimp caught. (NOAA)".

The Gulf dead zone is about 8776 square miles, varying year to year, about the size of New Jersey. The distribution of the dead zone extends from the vicinity of the mouth of the river, westward to offshore central Texas. Most of the area has an oxygen level at the seafloor of less than 2 mg/l.

The dead zone threatens the commercial and recreational fisheries of the Gulf, valued at almost $1 billion. It also drives up the price of large shrimp relative to smaller sizes, causing economic ripples that can affect consumers, fishermen and seafood markets alike." The Nature Conservancy has been working with farmers to precisely limit the quantity and quality of soil amendments to achieve a decrease in volume that does not hinder crop production, and to seek cover crops that are profitable but are more effective at soil conservation. Such efforts that are paying off, and when expanded, will pay benefits for centuries throughout the impact area. The economic benefits would reach the end stage consumer of Gulf fisheries. (The Nature Conservancy, Stopping the Cycle of Dead Zones in the Gulf of Mexico and Beyond, August 03, 2017, Justin Adams and Larry Clemens)

Drinking Water from the Big Muddy

The city of New Orleans gets its water from the Mississippi River. "The water enters the Carrollton Water Purification Plant from two large pumping stations. The purification process begins with the addition of coagulant chemicals. These chemicals cause fine particles or solids in the river water to clump together. Once the river water has coagulated, it is gently mixed by mechanical paddles. This process of flocculation causes the fine particles that were created during coagulation to mature into larger particles that will quickly settle into holding basins. The flocculated water then travels into primary settling basins, where the large, dense particles settle, allowing the clarified water to be separated and forwarded on through the remainder of the water treatment process. Sludge on the bottom of the basins is periodically removed. The clarified water is disinfected with the addition of chlorine. Ammonia is then added, producing chloramine. The chloramine-disinfected water passes through a second set of basins to provide time for the disinfection process to complete. Lime, also known as calcium oxide, is added to achieve the desired target pH. Adjusting the pH makes the water more basic, and less corrosive to the pipes in the water distribution system and the plumbing in homes and businesses. A small amount of polyphosphate is also added with the lime, which helps to keep the lime dissolved in the water" (Dan Swenson, NOLA. com, The Times Picayune, September 13, 2014.

This purified and cleaned up water then enters a rotting pipeline system for the most part. The water pressure must be maintained by pumps to an exacting level or better to ascertain that water flows outward through the leaks rather than inward. If the water pressure in the pipes gets too low, this leaking process is reversed and the groundwater, which may not be fit to drink, enters the water supply. The city then puts out a boil water advisory. Having to boil the water you use, then cool it when necessary, for all purposes, is a horrendous process which probably is not followed assiduously. To the city's credit, they usually get out a supply of good water in jugs or boxes given away in the affected area. There is advice online about how to add chlorine (bleach) to water for purification if boiling is not feasible.

New Orleans is between the Mississippi River to the south and Lake Pontchartrain to the north. Both pose flooding threats to the city that is protected to some extent by levees. As for the river, in times of flooding, the crest, that is the highest point of flow that is progressing downstream, is carefully tracked. It may be determined that if a crest is moving toward the city at a level that may top the levees, some of the water is diverted from the river at the Bonnie Carre Spillway which is a few miles upstream from New Orleans. The lake is brackish, but still suitable for many saltwater species, trout, shrimp, and crabs. This diversion puts sediment laden fresh water into the lake and all downstream waterways. This is not an attractive nor desirable situation for those affected, but it does clear up some weeks after the event. Then we are blessed with freshwater catfish in salt water.

CHAPTER 10

THE LEVEE SYSTEM

The levee system protects the city of New Orleans up to a certain height of storm surge. Raising the height and improving it overall has been going on since Katrina. It is much improved. Whether it will be adequate for whatever nature may hurl at New Orleans is in the future.

The onslaught of the levees comes from all directions. From the north, the Tangipahoa and Tchefuncte rivers, and from the west, rivers flowing into and out of Lake Maurepas, swollen by torrential rains at times, enter Lake Pontchartrain to raise the lake level and assault the levees on the north side of the city. The Mississippi River bounds New Orleans to the south. From this direction there is the possibility that a storm surge in the Gulf, as with Katrina, can bring oceanic waters to the city, as well as storm waters coming down the rivers. From the east, Lake Borgne, which practically speaking is a bay of the Gulf, with its associated vast marshes, comes right up to the levees. Calculations as to what to do with the levees has been going on for a long time. People live outside the levees in all directions. Inside the New Orleans levee bowl most likely will not flood at all due to improvements in levee construction, storm gates, and increasing the height that have continued ever since Katrina.

The risk to the city and surrounding areas has been worsened by bad planning and canal construction that never should have been. The biggest boondoggle was the construction of the Mississippi River Gulf Outlet. That is "Mister Go" to us natives. This is a straight ship-capable canal from the gulf right up to the city. It hastened storm surges right up and into the city. It has now been blocked at one point by a porous stone ridge, post Katrina. A gigantic solid wall barrier has been built near where mister go nears New Orleans. This barrier is explained in Wikipedia as follows; "The Inner Harbor Navigation Canal Lake Borgne Surge Barrier is a storm surge barrier constructed near the confluence of and across the Gulf Intracoastal Waterway (GIWW) and the Mississippi River Gulf Outlet (MRGO) near New Orleans. The barrier runs generally north-south from a point just east of Michoud Canal on the north bank of the GIWW and just south of the existing Bayou Bienvenue flood control structure. Navigation gates where the barrier crosses the GIWW and Bayou Bienvenue reduce the risk of storm surge coming from Lake Borgne and/or the Gulf of Mexico. Another navigation gate (Seabrook Floodgate) has been constructed in the Seabrook vicinity where the IHNC meets Lake Pontchartrain to block a storm surge from entering the IHNC from the Lake." These changes have lessened risk for the city, and changed salt water to fresh for areas that previously were salt.

CHAPTER 11

PiLOTTOWN AND THE RiVER PiLOTS ASSOCiATiON

Pilottown is beyond the end of the southbound road that runs down the river delta toward the Gulf. It is the historical departure point for pilots, bar pilots to guide ships through the passes from the Gulf to the Head of Passes, and river pilots to take it from Pilottown to New Orleans and beyond. Head of Passes is considered the mouth of the Mississippi River. From this location, proceeding toward the Gulf, there are three main passes and numerous other passes. Passes tend to be treacherous, requiring careful and informed pilotage. The Southwest Pass has come to be the preferred entry to the mouth of the river. For those who work from Pilottown, no road is available. Bar pilots will go to the ship in the Gulf. Ships may be boarded by climbing up a 30-foot ladder or perhaps by helicopter.

Pilottown was well developed in the 1930's, with stores, bars, and permanent residents. Since Katrina it has become dilapidated, without permanent residents. The Pilots association has relocated from Pilottown to Venice, which is the end of the road. To get from there to Pilottown requires a boat or helicopter.

Ships in gulf waters bound for New Orleans and beyond via the Mississippi River are required by law to hire the services of a river pilot. The pilot is a skilled captain intimately familiar with the channel of some segment of the river. The four pilot associations are described in Wikipedia as follows: "On the Lower Mississippi River, the Associated Branch Pilots supplies River Pilots between the Gulf of Mexico and Pilottown, Louisiana. The Crescent River Port Pilots Association supplies River Pilots between Pilottown and New Orleans, Louisiana, and the New Orleans-Baton Rouge Steamship Pilots Association supplies River Pilots between New Orleans and Baton Rouge, Louisiana. The Associated Federal Pilots and Docking Masters of Louisiana are pilots who deal strictly with US Flagged vessels and operate from Southwest Pass to Baton Rouge, the longest transit of the 4 pilot associations in the river." Pilotage fees are applied separately for each river segment, going and coming. So, from the gulf to Baton Rouge six pilotage fees would accrue, in and out.

"Together, the three Mississippi River groups make up the largest collection of state-commissioned pilots in the United States. Of the 1,100 state pilots who work the nation's ports and inland waterways, about 230 work on the Mississippi River in Louisiana". (Masters of the River | NOLA.com Aug 10, 2016)

This setup, where ships must have a river pilot from one of the associations or be penalized, has been the subject of much media attention, largely in the negative sense. For this reason, it is useful to examine the legal basis in law that defines the system.

River Port Pilot Statutes

LA R.S. 34:991 et. seq. included the following language, which is excerpted for relevance from the lengthier provisions.

"There is hereby created the Board of River Port Pilot Commissioners for the Port of New Orleans. The board shall consist of three citizens appointed by the governor, with the consent of the Senate, who presently hold a commission as a river port pilot and such commission has been active for a period of not less than four years. The governor, in appointing the said commissioners, shall designate the president of the board. The commissioners shall serve at the pleasure of the governor.

The river port pilots shall have the exclusive right to pilot vessels on the Mississippi River between New Orleans, Louisiana and Pilottown, Louisiana and within the Port of New Orleans between Southport and Mereauxville; within the Industrial Canal, between the Mississippi River to and including Lake Pontchartrain; within the Intracoastal Canal, between the Industrial Canal and the turning basin at Michoud, inclusive; also for the Mississippi River Gulf Outlet between the Industrial Canal and Mile 28.3, the Gulf Intracoastal Waterway from the Louisiana-Mississippi state line to the Mississippi River Gulf Outlet, including Michoud Slip and Michoud Canal, Chef Pass, Algiers Cutoff, and the Harvey Canal; the Venice Jump within six and one-half miles of the Mississippi River; Bayou Sauvage; and Bayou Liberty."

"The river port pilots shall be entitled to ask for and to receive a fee for their pilotage services. The fees for pilotage services shall be established in accordance with R.S. 34:1121, et seq. All vessels shall employ a river port pilot when navigating the operating territory described in this Subpart except those vessels exempted by the laws of the United States or vessels of one hundred gross tons or less. In case of refusal to take such river port pilot, the master, owner, agent, or consignee of any vessel required to employ a river port pilot shall pay the established pilot fee as if a river port pilot had been employed. "

"Anyone attempting to exercise the functions herein vested in the said river port pilots, who has not been commissioned by the governor, shall be fined not less than one thousand five hundred dollars, nor more than five thousand dollars, or imprisoned not less than thirty days, nor more than four months, or both, at the discretion of the court in whose jurisdiction the offense is committed."

"No master, owner, or agent of a vessel required under this Subpart to take a state commissioned river port pilot shall perform the duties of a river port pilot nor employ a person who is not a state commissioned river port pilot. Whoever violates this Section shall be fined not less than one thousand five hundred dollars nor more than five thousand dollars, or imprisoned for not more than six months, or both."

"The Pilotage Fee Commission shall exist to establish pilotage fees. The commission shall be composed of eleven members and nine alternates. The governor shall appoint the members…"

Three at-large members and one at-large alternate… shall sign and maintain a statement of neutrality and shall not be a family member of nor have a financial, business, or pecuniary relationship with a member or with any entity represented on the commission or on the Board of Louisiana River Pilot Review and Oversight. No at-large member shall have any ex parte communication with any member of any pilot association or with any member of the nominating industry groups or any other person or entity that has an interest in any issue pending before the commission except for educational purposes"

The Controversy

Last year the average Bar Pilot made $586,000, Crescent Pilots an average $595,000 and NOBRA pilots $633,000. We've (Zurik and Wright) uncovered a letter that likely has never been seen by the general public - one that impacts a handful of well-connected Louisianans earning more than half a million dollars a year. The river pilots are also able to earn additional money through a transportation tariff, traveling to and from work. Records reviewed by FOX 8 show one river pilot made $758,000 last year. This pilot is part of the New Orleans Baton Rouge Steamship Pilots Association, or NOBRA. Records show that can top $40,000 a year, additional money going to the pilots. Essentially, the pilots are paid even to drive to work. (Lee Zurik and Tom Wright, WVUE, Fox8, August 10, 2018.) This is the basis of controversy for decades of stress over alleged excesses and lack of oversight for a process defined by statute.

The letter Zurick and Wright refer to, dated March 16, 2016, is from Captain Stephen H. Hathorn, President, New Orleans-Baton Rouge Steamship Pilots Association, to Governor John Bel Edwards. On behalf of the association, Captain Hathorn recommends three individuals to serve as at-large members of the pilotage fee commission, as follows: Lenora A. Cousin, Daniel W. Kingston, and as Chair, Bruce G. Mohon. The governor picked all three members to serve on the commission.

"They're the key on the board," Bowser president of the Louisiana Chemical Association.", says. "Something's wrong. They're the swing votes, if you will. We've spent several months investigating this commission; we've spoken to many sources connected to the businesses and the river pilots. When we asked one source - who asked for anonymity - about the current commission, that person told us, "It's fixed." Another told us, "The Pilotage Fee Commission has been corrupted... It's a lock for the pilots because the system has been manipulated.""

"State law says these independents need to be neutral parties; they cannot be connected to the river pilots or the industries those pilots serve. They essentially decide where each vote before the board goes, who wins, who loses, who makes money, who pays up. But they're not supposed to be tied to either industry or river pilots".

"Playing politics with commission appointments is not new to Edwards. He appointed three members to a commission regulating the salaries of Louisiana river pilots. Edwards got the names and résumés of his three appointees directly from an organization representing river pilots. Edwards was rewarded with six-figure campaign contributions from river pilots, their families, attorneys and lobbyists." (Dan Fagan. The Advocate, August 28, 2018."

"We're not here to say that Zurik's sources calling that commission corrupt are 100 percent right. What we can say, though, is this stuff matters – Louisiana has some of the busiest ports in the world by an accident of geography, but even so those ports are not as busy or as lucrative as they could be – and

Louisiana loses business to Houston, Gulfport and Mobile in no small part because of shenanigans like what's in Zurik's report. There is a mentality here which holds that we don't have to do things the right way because "they have to be here" – whether "they" is oil companies, petrochemical plants, shipping or whatever industry is targeted as a mark by politicians and others. And for a long time that might even have been true. But in the 21st century it's less so. Commerce is easier now and the options are greater. The old-school Louisiana way, which Edwards clearly espouses with respect to the river pilots leads to ruin. He doesn't even try to defend himself in that Zurik interview; his response is essentially "so what?"." (The Hayride, MacAoidh, May 24, 2-018)

In lists of the most dangerous rivers in the world, the Mississippi is always noted. One one such list, titled "The Eight Most Dangerous Rivers in the World, Geo Hagan (The Richest, July 23, 2014) puts it this way:" At one stretch of its almost 2340 miles, the waters could be as mellow as a serene backyard pool, but then a couple of miles upstream or downstream, a sailor could be facing dangerous floating debris, risky riptides, and currents that could easily capsize any type of seaworthy vessel. For the most part, these large bodies of water are very similar to human beings. One day they are nice and inviting, and the next, they want to turn you upside down and have nothing to do with you."

Mark Twain had a lot to say about the dangers of this river. Richard Nordquist (Thoughtco, July 4, 2018) reported on Twain as follows in two ways of seeing a river. The romance and the beauty were all gone from the river. Twains writing delves into the changes in attitude about the river he experienced after becoming a steamboat pilot. In essence, it reveals the reality versus the myth of the majestic, Mighty Mississippi--revealing danger beneath the mesmerizing beauty that could only be discovered by taking to the river itself.

It is clear that the river is challenging to navigation, that a mishap could have dire consequences far beyond the particular vessel involved, and that piloting is a skill that requires exhaustive preparation and is a stressful and physically demanding profession. The question that haunts and maddens is, how to make sense of the three piloting association's salaries that are inarguably the most rewarding in the world for practitioners of this profession, clearly out of line with all other such associations in the United States.

A factor to consider is not just what happens after the pilot gets on the ship, a strange phenomenon where the pilot takes command of the ship, surrendered for this purpose by the captain of the ship, but how the pilot gets to the location where the ship is boarded, and gets back home with his transport after getting off the boat at the end of the one-way trip. This situation is entirely different from the ordinary commute to work, giving rise to the effort to compensate the pilot for all this aggravation in addition to his compensation for the piloting he or she provides.

In the latest dustup over pilot compensation, industry representatives demanded a justification for a further increase in pilot compensation. The associations refused to provide it. The matter went to court. The lawsuit contends that evidence of pilot control includes a vote on whether to boost the transportation rates for getting pilots on and off of boats by 40 percent — about $98,000. The neutral members sided with the pilots in deciding there was no need for evidence to support the increase, a decision later reversed by the 19th District. (Chemical shippers sue agency that sets river pilots' pay. The Associated Press, January 1, 2019)

In addition to the compensation issues, the amounts and approval process, there is incessant but unrequited anger about the closed society of the three river associations. Family and friends are the prerequisites. Outsiders cannot breach this barrier no matter their qualifications. "Under state law, river pilots enjoy virtually unfettered control over who is admitted to their small fraternity, whose members enjoy a monopoly on the job of guiding foreign vessels along the lower Mississippi. About 230 pilots help guide the ships from the mouth of the Mississippi to ports as far upriver as Baton Rouge. Given the generous pay and modest working hours, the jobs are among the most desirable in the local maritime industry. They also are among the most exclusive. Of the 100 people elected to become river pilots in recent years, 85 are related to other pilots, and several who were granted the lucrative positions are the sons of state legislators or the nephews of a lobbyist, records show. "It's no wonder the jobs are kept in the family." (MacAoidh, Lee Zurik's Expose' on the River Pilots Is Required Viewing For Every Louisiana Voter May 24th, 2018.)

No matter how eloquent, any expressions of fair play and moral outrage will not whip this puppy. The system is defined by statute and immune from fine argument and persuasion. It is possible that the law as written could work fairly for all, but not in Louisiana. Any factions wanting to change this system will have to generate the will and backing to change the law, and that has not happened yet, hence it is what the Louisiana political system decrees.

CHAPTER 12

NASA MiCHOUD ASSEMBLY FACiLiTY

Sitting in a boat on Lake Borgne, more practically speaking it should be Borgne Bay, looking west, one thing dominates the horizon 12 miles away—the huge windowless cube of a building at the Michoud facility. New Orleans skyscrapers are marginally imposing a few miles further west. This facility is located on the intracoastal waterway, the wet highway used to move the fuel tanks manufactured there to the launch facility at Cape Canaveral, Florida. This is done by barge and tug around the tip of Florida and north to the cape. This is a 1000-mile trip in a covered barge, giving it more sea time than air time. The tank, at 154 feet, was taller than the Statue of Liberty (151 feet) and was the structural backbone of the shuttle vehicle. There were approximately 480,000 separate parts in each external tank. The external tank held 535,000 gallons of propellants -- 390,000 gallons liquid hydrogen and 145,000 gallons liquid oxygen -- which fuel space shuttle main engines through 17-inch-diameter feedlines. (NASA.gov).

In 2013, the facility was "Managed and operated by NASA's Marshall Space Flight Center in Huntsville, Alabama. Michoud built the Saturn S-1C and Saturn S-1B boosters for the Apollo program, and the large external tank for the shuttle program. It now is building the Orion spacecraft. The facility is being modified to manufacture the core stage of NASA's Space Launch System rocket, the most powerful ever built." (Trent J. Perrotto, Angela Storey, and Chip Howat. NASA'S Michoud Assembly Facility Manufactures Liquid Natural Gas Tanks for Lockheed Martin. NASA.gov. March 12, 2013). Later they were to change management to a facility manager separate from the prime contractors.

The final launch of the space shuttle discovery was February 24, 2011. The YouTube video of this flight shows the configuration, that is the fuel tank, the two rockets attached to the fuel tank, and the shuttle attached also, as it ascends from the thrust of the two rockets attached to the fuel tank, with the shuttle inert along for the ride at this point. The first detachments after two minutes are the two solid fuel rocket boosters attached to the fuel tank. When the boosters burn deplete fuel, they detach, fall to ocean with a parachute, are recovered and reused. Later the fuel tank detaches and disintegrates in the atmosphere, at which time the engines on the shuttle take over and it is on its way. (STS-133 The Final Launch of Space Shuttle Discovery including T-5 hold Published on Mar 9, 2011}

The last flight qualified tank built was destined for a long trip by sea to wind up in a museum in Los Angeles. This involved putting it on a covered barge, departing New Orleans Michoud facility and heading for the Panama Canal, then north up the west coast to the city. From there it was moved on city streets to its final location, the California Science Center after a 4,400-mile trip that took one month.

The Orion spacecraft is the only mission currently being developed for deep space, mars and beyond, and return. It is being built by Lockheed Martin at the Michoud Facility. It is now at the end of the exploratory stage and primed for a mission in 2020, followed by the first crewed mission in 2022. (Matt Williams, Construction on the Orion Capsule is Done Universe Today, August 29, 2018)

"NASA is assembling the major components of its Orion crew capsule and Space Launch System at Michoud. Other initiatives at the facility include development of liquid oxygen and liquid hydrogen tanks for the SLS, a deep-space rocket that will propel the capsule into space on a test flight. NASA eventually plans to send a crew and cargo on Orion, leading to more work for Michoud to develop a larger portion of the rocket. "(CityBusiness staff reports. New jobs, college training program set for Michoud facility. November 1, 2017)

CHAPTER 13

EXPANDiNG FROM LAND TO SEA

P robably the most famous image of oil discovery in the world is the 1901 Spindletop gusher, an enormous geyser pictured shooting 150 feet into the sky and drenching the site in oil. This was in southeast Texas, the genesis of a booming oil industry in the area, the beginnings of many oil companies in this country that still exist.

From this land-based origin, man and equipment worked its way south in Louisiana, into marshes, into shallow water, into intermediate water depth, and finally the last frontier, deep water. Now, operators are going into ultra-deep water. Deep water by definition is only 400 meters at minimum. There are projects with water depth of 3000 meters and above. Challenges are abundant as the water depth is increased. The main issues are high pressure and high temperature which require the planning, analysis and review by qualified professionals in the field, as well as verification by consultants and other third-party reviews.

The equipment and methods evolved in accordance. Barges were used in shallow water and marshes, giving way to jackup rigs in shallow waters, to floating rigs in deeper water, and platforms on high pedestals anchored to the seafloor, these resembling the fire towers we see ashore, with the workings 50 feet or so over the water, the remaining structure under water. In the deepest waters, massive anchoring assemblages stretch out like an eight-legged spider, managed by winches on the platforms that have spools as big as a house, and cable lengths that span many miles. In one famed illustration of the deepest such anchoring, the platform, or rig was pictured as over city of Houston, with the anchoring system to scale, which could be seen to encompass the entire city, if it were magically hovered overhead.

On my first day in the office, my Deputy, a very honorable guy, Dr. Richard Defenbaugh, said to me: "Hammond, I want to warn you, do not say rig when referring to those structures in the gulf, unless it is a rig. You will identify yourself as a complete novice to one an all if you do that. A rig is a drilling rig. It drills. It is the first structure on a site. After a discovery, or a dry hole is established, the rig moves off and a platform is put over the productive hole. A platform is for production. A rig is for exploration and establishing a producing well head. Most of the structures out there are platforms and if you err in this you are going to be wrong, wrong, wrong". Ok, I have elaborated on this a bit past what Rick actually said, but it made quite the impression.

In Spindletop, one gets the impression that the entirety of the operation is pictured in the one photograph. From such a beginning, multi-disciplined companies grew, and from that multi private contractors and consultants grew, until now the operation includes rentals of rigs, various contractors working as needed, and exhaustive use of high-tech communications. The technicians and brain trust of a company may be housed on land, in constant contact with the offshore component by ongoing examination of every aspect of the operation via high tech transmissions of images and data from the offshore operation. On the drilling rig, many images of the progress of the drilling are produced, including data regarding pressure, temperature, grouting or whatever has bearing on the success and safety of the operation. Since the Deepwater Horizon incident, BSEE (the Bureau of Safety and Environmental Enforcement) has substantially tightened its permitting requirements in drilling operations, well design, bottom hole pressure testing, emergency plans, etc. Any changes to the approved plan will have to be thoroughly reviewed again. Submittal of weekly activity reports are made to show any progress on drilling and any issues a company might have encountered. BSEE also has regulations for mobile offshore drilling units (MODU) for drilling and testing. If communication is lost between MODU and the rig or platform while drilling or producing, valves will be shut down and the operator will have to notify BSEE for further action.

Technicians for the host company, for all the contractors, on land, on water, are involved. If it is a disaster, there would lots of blame to go around. If contractors, or any element involved, is hell bent on profits, uses inferior materials, cuts short on rental fees, fails to test the safety equipment such as the rams on blowout preventers, or proper cement bonding, it may not be known to all parties. The quest for guilty parties when something goes awry is tedious and very technical.

Lessons learned from the Deepwater Horizon disaster, especially the huge fines, have led to changes in operational methods by both oil companies and contractors. Knowing that BSEE is closely scrutinizing every aspect of the operation and is being reinforced by the expertise of the Houston Engineering Technology Center, with personnel hired mostly from the industry, operators are leery of being caught in unsafe practices no matter how small.

CHAPTER 14

GULF OF MEXiCO MiNERAL RESOURCE DEVELOPMENT

The earliest oil well known was in China in 347 ad, 790 feet deep. In the 9th century, wells were developed in Baku, Azerbaijan. The first well in North America was in Ontario in 1858, and the first offshore well was off California in 1896. Percussive drilling was used until it was replaced by rotary drilling in the 20th century. After the 1970's, horizontal drilling was added to the oilman's repertoire, or the oil woman's, if there were any. Products of a well include crude oil, propane, butane, methane, and possibly hydrogen sulfide, which is extremely toxic and may cause death by damaging lung cells.

Oil and gas exploration and development is regulated by state and federal agencies. Authority rests with the adjacent states out to 3 miles, with the exception of Florida and Texas (9 miles), and beyond that is the federal government. The responsible federal agency was the Minerals Management Service up until it was reorganized into two agencies following the Deepwater Horizon disaster. Thus, three federal agencies, the United States Coast Guard, the Bureau of Safety and Environmental Enforcement, and the Bureau of Ocean Energy Management now hold jurisdiction. We will leave the bureaucratic designation with that, and henceforth just call it the fed.

"Since the first offshore drilling began in 1942, about 6,000 oil and gas structures have been installed in the Gulf of Mexico. These structures range in size from single well caissons in 10-ft water depths to large, complex facilities in water depths up to almost 10,000 ft. About 3,500 structures currently stand in the Gulf of Mexico; of these, over 3,200 remain active".(NOAA Gulf of Mexico Data Atlas)

An overview of the activities under federal jurisdiction include private companies operating as of this date, 57 drilling rigs. There are an estimated 13,000 miles of active pipelines and about 27,000 miles of abandoned pipelines. About 12,000 people work offshore, supported by another 50,000 onshore in this industry, for a total of 62,000. (Lori Ann LaRocco, CNBC.com, February 10, 2011). Subfloor drilling can go to 35,000 feet for some rigs in more shallow water, and some can operate in water depth out to 12,000 feet. Offshore workers travel mostly by helicopter to the structures. Lots of supply boats ply the waters to transport industrial materials and support for those living on the structures. Most of the hydrocarbons are moved from the platforms to shore in a pipe. Pipe inspections internally are done by smart pigs. That is a cylindrical data gathering instrument shaped somewhat like a big medicinal capsule. It hosts lots of instrumentation for gathering data on pipeline condition. Put it in a pipe 20 miles offshore and it pops out at the other end on land. It is pushed along by pressure from the platform. There are pressure gauges at intervals along the pipeline to denote pressure drops that may be caused by leaks, thus leading to repairs at specific spots.

The feds operate a system that awards leases for mineral development, specific to depth and horizontal geographic boundaries. In this system, areas to be leased are identified geographically, advertised, and bid on via 2 or 3 big lease auctions held in French Quarter hotels and attended by hundreds of industry participants. The leases go to the highest bidders, and beyond that, the lessee pays royalties to the fed on the production. The royalty is some fraction of the production. Various grades of oil are produced, as well as various gasses like butane and propane. A well may have quite an assortment of hydrocarbons recovered. Sometimes small amounts of gasses are not economically feasible to recover and may be burned at sea in flares, which are big pipes sticking off the production platforms, ignited, and burning and smoking day and night.

The fed has lots of highly qualified personnel, many in the environmental field with PhDs in every discipline that applies. Many in the engineering fields have appropriate degrees, as do those in the financial and legal provinces. Whatever may be or may have been wrong in this system does not attribute to the quality of the workers. It attributes to national attitudes, motives, biases, backgrounds, and aspirations of the highest leadership in the US government, right up to the President of the United States.

When I entered this system, in 1998, George W. Bush was President and Chris Oynes was the Regional Director. The various large categories of responsibility included engineering, permitting, oil and gas resource assessment, leasing, oceanic environment, enforcement, and financial management aspects. My job was involved with oceanic environment, leasing and permitting.

The system and interactions among these persons and disciplines had been in place for a long time. That led to complacence. Being a novice in this group of seasoned oil and gas federal people, and responsible for environmental reviews of what was to happen with the exploration and development activity, I soon asked, "what happens if we have a major blowout?" The question was assigned to the engineering sector, who in a couple of weeks came back with "That is impossible". We have multiram blowout preventers on every pipe. The technology is so advanced that the ram would never even be needed. And so on. This position did not lead to approaching the fed role in disaster prevention as a critical matter. The spill containment resources of the industry were assessed by someone in the environmental side, and resented by those in the engineering side since the attitude was that it never would be needed. Besides, the industry led in the technology, which is akin to the space program, and was always ahead of the fed in understanding the technology and performance of the equipment.

The enforcement sector was to be cognizant of threats and equipment failures, and spills. This fell under the engineering sector. The performance of the industry was to be made known through the engineering and inspection and enforcement activities. This was to be made public to all, including those of us within the system. This failed. In the media examination of the Deepwater Horizon disaster, we in the fed learned that much had been going wrong without our knowledge. For instance, there were lots of spills. Who knew? Nothing like Deepwater Horizon, however.

A massive flaring far offshore, pumping so much flame and smoke that viewed from space via satellite there were three apparent geologic events outstanding on earth--two volcanoes and an oil company flaring far out of sight offshore. The flaring was so bad that an environmental staff guy happened upon it by accident and observed that the sky was blackened from horizon to horizon. This led to examination of the permit which failed to address it, of the inspection that failed to address it, to assessment of personal liability on the part of industry persons, to resistance within the fed to dealing with any enforcement activity, to admonitions to remain silent while the situation was studied. As years passed and I tried to find out what happened with this, no one was talking. I was advised that this position was coming from the fed in DC.

Rocking along as in years past, this system was rocked by President George W. Bush, who ordered that the oil and gas industry would be enforced by self-reporting. This was akin to the government declaring that all people involved in traffic violations must report themselves to authorities who would not be on the road doing enforcement, and submit to the subsequent punishment meted out. When this first came out, I just could not figure out how it was supposed to work in some successful fashion. Reading an Inspectors General's report on this, it turns out that the industry permittee used government inspection forms to fill out in pencil the findings of an inspection that was never conducted. That form was given to the government inspector who wrote over it in ink to produce the official record. I am not ready to believe, however, that this was the prevailing method. Just how widespread this practice was not in the report.

President George W. Bush defined the direction of this federal regulatory agency at this point. Clearly, production was the goal. The assumption and belief were that industry was so advanced in technology and self-interest that a blowout or big spill was an impossibility. Knowing that a big pollution event would be sensational news, hyped to the hilt by a media seeking viewers, a wave of negativity would sweep the nation and severely damage the bottom line of the offshore oil and gas industry, so in self-interest if for no other reason the industry would never let it happen, it was generally believed. That was the regulatory atmosphere under which Chris Oynes operated. He died in Baton Rouge in 2017, and I am a bit saddened by that. Chris was a lawyer. He was not an engineer, nor a biologist. He viewed his job as a "noble mission". Bring energy resources on line in the USA to the benefit of all, and break the stranglehold the foreign producers are trying to exercise over the world.

It is a curious thing that lawyers are routinely put in charge of federal agencies. All too frequently what they bring to the table is ignorance about the specifics of the resources under their jurisdiction, placed there as a political accommodation. Chris was a lovable person and a smart lawyer. His commitment to production and his belief in the infallibility and ethics of the industry created a work environment that was hostile to the environmental knowledge and skills of his staff. And, he did not recognize that he was neither a biologist nor an engineer, so there were no boundaries that threatened his self-assessment of his capabilities. Being the most skillful bureaucrat in the agency, he could and did bend it to his will. This was evidenced by his being put in an advanced position after the Deepwater Horizon disaster, when the agency splintered into two other agencies.

CHAPTER 15

THE SEAFLOOR

T he Gulf seafloor is mainly sand and mud. There are ridges and canyons offering some topographic diversity. Some really strange things are in limited supply, making them easy to avoid in any bottom disturbance. This includes creatures living on deep sea gas vents, naturally occurring leaks of methane. Here is where hundred-year-old tube worms are found, as well as clams and some other interesting life. Some life forms consume 90 percent of the methane coming from the vents, thus helping in the reduction of greenhouse gasses. The seafloor is littered with wrecks of archaeological and historic value. Some old wooden wrecks were dated by MMS marine archaeologists by the fact that copper bottoms were nailed on with galvanized nails, putting the date within a 100-year time span, which ended when it was observed that the galvanized nails rusted.

Coast Guard Patrol Vessel Sinks German U-Boat

A German predatory submarine was stationed off the mouth of the Mississippi River for years during World war II, sinking passenger ships such as the Robert E. Lee, and vessels being built by Gulf shipbuilding companies and being tested in waters of the Gulf. The submarine did not return to Germany after the war and was lost to history until it was found by a Shell

Offshore oil company seafloor survey prior to putting a pipeline down. There was much controversy about how it got sunken, much high browed naval expertise asserting that it could not have been sunk by the depth charge as asserted by the captain of the US Coast Guard patrol boat accompanying the Robert E. Lee. That position was posited upon assumptions as to what depth the charge was set for, and what depth the sub was operating at when it fired its torpedoes. WWII German submarines had a collapse depth of 660 to 920 feet depth. It was therefore assumed that the depth charge was set for hundreds of feet depth, but dropped by the Coast Guard when the sub was near the surface immediately after its attack on the passenger ship. Therefore, the navy concluded that the Coast Guard did not sink the sub. That position stuck as far as history is concerned until the oil company marine archaeologists produced side scan survey images that showed that the sub was resting on the seafloor in two parts: The front third of the sub had been blown off.

Thus, history has been revised. On July 30, 1942, a United States Coast Guard 173-foot Patrol Craft sank German U-boat 166 off the coast of Louisiana, out from the mouth of the Mississippi River. The depth charge, which the coast guard dropped, came to rest and lodged on the forward deck of the sub. The explosive remained inert until the sub retreated to the depths, at which time the charge exploded, severing the forward portion of the submarine. Upon being informed of the discovery of the sub, the German government took the position that it was a NAZI submarine and would remain on the seafloor in obscurity in an undisclosed location without ceremony.

This event is recorded in the Patrol Craft Sailors Association records as follows: "PC 566 Sank German U-Boat, Gulf of Mexico 07-30-42." The Navy rejected reports 72 years ago that Lt. Cmdr. Herbert Claudius sank a German U-boat off the Louisiana coast during World War II. In fact, Officials criticized his depth-charging tactics and sent him to anti-submarine school so he could learn how to do it the right way. It turns out the Navy — not Claudius — was off target. Navy Secretary Ray Mabus and Chief of Naval Operations Adm. Jon Greenert set the record straight Dec. 16, when they posthumously awarded the Legion of Merit with combat "V" to the patrol coastal skipper. His son, Herbert Gordon Claudius Jr., received the award on behalf of his father. (Lance Bacon, Navy Times, December 22, 2014).

Seafloor Surveys Required

Such seafloor surveys are required by the fed and conducted by the industry prior to all bottom disturbance. Most anything down there above the mud-line will be found and handled in accord with historic preservation requirements by regulation and law.

CHAPTER 16

WHALES

There are a couple of dozen or so species of whales and dolphins in the Gulf of Mexico at some time of year. Motoring out of Gulfport, Mississippi, on the Tommy Monroe with the marine mammal class from the University of Southern Mississippi, getting out there about 80 miles, you get in sperm whale territory. Look for spouts. Sperm whales float low in the water and are hard to spot for that reason. Also, unlike most whales that spout straight, the sperm whale blows left and forward. Off in the distance you can tell from the spout if it is a sperm. One may wonder how these huge mammals can be subject to harvesting by harpoons thrown by hand. Well, puttering up on a female and calf just wallowing around and sloshing in the light waves, it was apparent that we could get right up by them if we so chose. Keeping pace, engine running, I wondered just how asleep this girl was. All of a sudden, she realized she had a neighbor, blew out her bowels, threw up her tail, and smacked the water. The water in the area turned brown and was laden with squid beaks. The calf was curious as to what we were, and in the crystal-clear water decided to swim under the boat, belly up. Upside down does not seem to exist in whale vocabulary. One position is about as up as the opposite position, in terms of their apparent comfort. If you want to come off as erudite, start calling a group of dolphins a herd. Whales grouped are called a pod. You won't be wrong to call the dolphins a pod also

Whales emit low frequency sound waves that can cross oceans, possibly detectable by other whales as far as 10,000 miles. Sonar is a vital aspect of their physiology and life habits, critical to feeding success and navigation. An ongoing concern with all who deal with impacts of industrial activities in the ocean is, how does the noise added to the whale habitat affect the whale.

The offshore oil industry uses seismic surveys extensively to define subsurface strata and identify likely oil deposits. Early surveys on land used dynamite to create a shock wave which would travel downward through the strata and produce echoes from each stratum that would be received by instruments on the surface for interpretation and for computer analysis. For oceanic surveys now an air gun is used to produce the sound wave. The streamer array towed behind the survey vessel will be anywhere from 3 to 12 km long. The instrumentation on this array provides the data the oil company uses for exploration to find more oil.

As we try to figure out what to worry about regarding the whales, worrying about these seismic surveys makes perfect sense. Presumptions about impacts are troublesome and require scientific scrutiny if only we could define a reliable investigatory method. Even without knowing, we want to minimize the potential. Current methods involve avoiding seismic actions when marine mammals are in the vicinity. In the vicinity means detectable, that means, can a trained observer see them, which relies entirely on visibility conditions, or can instrumentation on the survey vessel detect them. If so, the operation is shut down until the animals move on.

Overall, the state of research determinations on this is weak and contradictory. Whales have repeatedly been observed approaching a seismic operation with no apparent concern. But does that mean there is no impact? We do not know. In a desperate effort to define a possible impact, the "rock concert hypothesis" has been floated. It has been shown, so this goes, that humans will voluntarily attend a rock concert where the music or whatever it may be called is so loud that it damages human hearing. In short, humans are so stupid they will go to a sound that will hurt them. So, we posit that is true. Then we propose that a whale is as stupid as a human. And there you have it. Whales swim into the array impact zone and get their sonar apparatus damaged, or so this theory suggests. Then what, shut down noises in the ocean worldwide. We have whales, we have seismic operations, and there is no definite conflict that can be made of it, under the mitigations that are now employed.

CHAPTER 17

JOYS AND TRiBULATiONS OF LONG-DiSTANCE SAiLiNG

If you are going to go out there and take a beating it's best to do it when you are younger, generally speaking.

Our steel, homemade Bruce Roberts spray sailboat was tethered with sliding hoops to two especially tall pilings at our dock here near New Orleans, on a salt water canal. When the inevitable storm would come, the boat would rise up on the pilings and no harm would come. Katrina came, with a storm surge that reached the second level of our house. Armordillo rose over the tops of the pilings and was blown against the house at the second level. In the pounding of the boat against the house, the boat tore off the second-floor deck railings on the house, tore off the deck, and caved in the dining room wall, on the second floor.

Months later the insurance company, Progressive, in our conversation, asked if I knew where the boat was, suggesting that most likely I did not know where it was. In fact, I did not know what happened to it. Progressive said they would pay out full value and we could get on with our lives. They sent a salvage crew out, got the boat, and we never saw it again.

We bought a Westsail 32, a full keel traditional, old fashioned sailboat, cutter rig, that is, one mainsail, two foresails, that had been berthed at a dock in Savannah, Georgia, largely unused for over 30 years; named "Bes", Egyptian goddess of pleasure. I went there and spend a month modernizing it, propane stove, refrigeration, roller furling on foresail (yankee, jib). Our son Jake volunteered to meet me in Savannah to begin a trip to New Orleans. He made an exploratory trip for a week in advance of the big trip to get coached on this particular boat and how to make it go.

Jake and his wife, Kathleen, a surgeon, and two sons, Ethan and Zachary, then about 4 years old, lived in Modesto, California. Dr. Eve, being of a fervent imagination, decided that since Jake could not be away from piloting passenger planes for United long enough to sail 2000 miles anywhere on a sailboat, we needed a plan. Her plan was, they rent a house on a remote island in the northern Abacos in the Bahamas, and she and their two sons would fly to Miami from San Francisco, and Sandra would fly to Miami from New Orleans and meet them, and they would get on an island hopper small plane and fly out to Marsh Harbor in the Abacos, and they would rent a motorboat and pile in with the kids and she would steer and Sandra would navigate and they would transit through islands and reefs and shoals and whatever and wind up on the small island where the rental house was, and Jake and I would depart Savannah on Bes to begin the 6 week journey to New Orleans by sailing the 500 miles to that island and we would all wind up there within the same month. Calculating how all this would mesh was too stupefying to fathom, so Jake and I decided to give it a week for our part.

Jake and I, trying to sleep in a bed in Savannah the day before departure, could not sleep. Neither of us could. We came to realize we were both awake and anxious to get moving, so we went to the boat and set sail in the dark, getting out to the sound and through Hell's gate in the dark and off to the south in the Intracoastal Waterway for our first milestone. We stayed in the Intracoastal Waterway from Savannah to Ft. Pierce, Florida. The coast along this path is a wonderful situation for sailing in the day and sleeping at anchor at night. These waters abound with anchorages and enthralling coastal marsh scenery. The sounds are regularly spaced so if you want to venture outside and south and back in for the night, that is certainly feasible and the water will clear up away from land and be beautiful. Downside of this is the shoals extend about 5 miles out before you can turn and run down the coast. Getting out and back in will add 10 miles to your trip. Insects are likely to be a problem at an anchorage.

There were two notable situations that are worth mentioning along the ICW route (Intracoastal Waterway). That would be, what happens when we transit the Kingsbay Naval Submarine Base near St. Marys, Georgia, just north of the Florida state line, and what happens when we go past the launch area at Cape Canaveral.

The submarine Base is the port for the Atlantic Fleet's Trident II Submarines. At the sub base vicinity, everything visible along our route was ordinary. We don't know when we got on it nor when we left, nor what a submarine did in these waters. At the point where we were sailing east, Atlantic Ocean visible through the main waterway from the ocean about a half mile ahead of us, suddenly the radio blared—"sailing vessel turn to starboard, sailing vessel turn to starboard". We looked around and could not see any other sailing vessel so we thought this message from the unknown might be for us so we turned to starboard. About a minute after that a US Navy RIB boat with machine guns pointed at us, obvious menace that we were, came speeding up and stayed off our port side in case instant intervention of our intentions might be needed.

Some distance behind the navy boat a rubber coated submarine showed up, motoring on the surface, crew in round hats with a little flat tassel hanging off the side, assembled in a formation on the rounded hull. As this passed by, Jake wondered if he could take a picture without getting shot so he started some sort of hand signal, point to the camera, point to the sub, get a quizzical look on his face, raise his hands helplessly to show he was not armed. This entertainment got him a thumbs up from the navy so he took some pictures.

Shortly after the sub passed, we had gotten even with the continuation of the ICW and turned south again. Jake was in the cabin at this point and noticed that he was standing in water. He looked out at me in the cockpit and announced, "Dad, we are sinking". We frantically switched places and I started pulling up floorboards trying to get to the bilge pump which was about 2.5 feet underwater and not visible for inspection. At this point a loud klaxon horn blared out such that it vibrated the boat and scared the hell out of both of us. We looked back and up at the bow of a freighter ship that was bearing down on us. I decided we needed to ground the boat to keep from sinking, so we turned to starboard to run it aground and get out of the way of the freighter.

The immediate problem was soon discovered, that is, what was wrong with the bilge pump. The switch for the pump, installed on construction years ago, was a flat, 3 position rocker switch screwed to the bulkhead beside the companionway to the cockpit, a place convenient to placing your hand. Looking at this switch, it was impossible to determine what position it was in. It was turned off. It probably was turned off ever since we departed from Savannah. It was long after that I determined where the water came in, a worrisome thing that haunted for weeks after that.

The propane locker, for safety reasons, where the tanks were stored, was in the stern, sealed from the interior and vented to the outside via holes in the hull about a foot above the waterline. When the boat was in a heavy wind, the bow would rise and the stern depress, and in this case, it put the vent holes underwater at times, so water flowed into the propane locker under these conditions. Since the propane locker was sealed, this should not have been a problem. But, long after this trip was over, I was determined to find out how the water got in the cabin, and discovered that there was an area of delamination in the hull where the vent holes were installed. This is just a one-inch hole drilled through the hull at that point. Water came in the vent hole, then into the delaminated opening, then into the interior. It would take quite a while for this to cause water over the floorboards. The bilge pump could have easily kept it pumped out and I would never have known about it except for the pump being switched off.

Passing through the Cape Canaveral area we saw nothing from the ICW related to launching rockets. We stopped at a large marina, lots of boats tied up, not a human being is sight, no store open, blistering heat, bright sun, nowhere to buy a popsicle. Some enormous manatees were lazily lolling around amongst the boats, water chrystal clear. We moved on, heading for Fr. Pierce, Florida, our point of departure from the United States.

A curious thing about boating on this waterway. From north Florida on south, there were lots of fairly large sailboats heading north. None were sailing; all were motoring. Most had a completely enclosed cockpit and most people on these boats wore coats. We thought it was hot, but maybe we were wrong about this, going by popular opinion. At one point someone along a developed waterway yelled at us that it was nice to see a sailboat sailing, as we were the only one doing so in quite a while.

We arrived in the harbor at Ft. Pierce in the early afternoon. The day was beautiful, the water clear and blue and green, the air balmy. The sensible thing to do here, and what most everyone does, is wait till dark to proceed across the Gulf Stream (the Stream) heading east toward the Bahamas, so you arrive after crossing the stream in the daylight and avoid slamming into something solid in the dark. Peachy keen day that it was, we decided we wanted to be in the Stream during the daylight and departed in good spirits.

The water in the Stream is clear and cobalt blue, as beautiful as water gets. It is about a half mile deep making this crossing. The water flows north, with a crest that has a flow rate of about 5 knots, tapering off to less as one approaches the shore. Heavy shipping rides this current north, as did early seafarers in wooden boats. Sandra and I made this crossing years earlier in

Armordillo, from Biscayne Bay just south of Miami, with a light wind, and a loran that said we were going 5 knots. Back then, Miami just would not drop below the horizon. The wind was light. How could we be going 5 knots, I wondered, pathetically. Then the light bulb came on, and I realized we were going 5 knots sideways, headed for the British Isles across the North Atlantic if I did not wake up.

Back aboard Bes, Jake and I needed to proceed southwest about 100 miles, destination West End vicinity, Grand Bahama Island. This angled us into the Stream which is a real setback as the Steam often goes faster than the boat. As darkness came on and we quartered against the Stream currents, the wind picked up, the waves picked up, and pitch-black darkness descended, apparently due to an overcast that developed. No light of any kind was to be seen anywhere. The absolute rule at this point is that everyone not in the cabin has to be tied to the boat. This is wearing a harness with a lanyard and carabiner that slides along fore and aft jacklines. Anyone going overboard in these conditions certainly could not be rescued or ever seen again from Bes. Jake and I both wore life jackets, ocean variety, and had waterproof flashlight tied to them, but one person trying to get that boat around and see a flashlight in towering waves was just a futile dream.

Around 3 am, a voice blared from Channel 16, the maritime emergency frequency, second time on this trip, "Turn around, Turn around". We could see no indication, no light, nothing to let us know what this was about, no way to know who they were calling. The voice never identified itself. We wondered if it were a warning that we were about to hit something or run aground or if there were some military thing going on in the dark or if we had stumbled into some drug related operation. We veered off course, more into the stream, which slowed us down even more, and heard nothing more of the voice from the dark. We kept a careful watch on the depth so as to warn us when we were getting out of the deep water That is often helpful, and certainly must be done, but not necessarily foolproof as some of the reefs rise from the depths over the span of just a few feet and present the equivalent of the brick wall 15 feet rising above the sea surface.

Daylight found us within the islands, north of West End, with about 150 miles to go through island and reef to get to Marsh Harbor, the destination of our hearty wives and young children before their final leg by outboard motor to another small island.

Jake and I checked in with customs and immigration, paid their tax of $300 for us to be there, and declared not much of anything except a .22 caliber pistol. They required a bullet count, which I thought I did and provided a number and went to sneak into the customs people's shower for a ….shower. In the meantime, Jake was left with the customs guy, who looked over the outside of the pistol with lazy curiosity, making everyone realize that he hardly knew what it was. Finishing the outside inspection of the gun, he wanted to count the bullets. So, he counted the little bullets and came out with more than I had come out with. Jake blamed his dad for the problem. No one knew what to do about this. Just change the number and move on is how it came out.

Having gotten that worrisome situation behind us, Jake and I anchored in the beautiful harbor, ready for an early departure next morning. The harbor was heavily populated with large sloops, two roller furled jibs or yankees each, inches apart, to carry heavy sail and light sail, which I was not used to as it is more expensive. People were sitting about here and there on the boats. Reading something, like the hyped beach novel. I wondered how many of them hoisted or unfurled sail and took to the waves and reefs, as we saw few boats on the water.

We took to sail at daylight the next day. About an hour out got slammed with a storm, high winds, rain so heavy we could not see land, thankful for the GPS or it would have been foolish to proceed. We later learned that the storm had overcome the anchored boats and pounded them against the shore facilities damaging both buildings and boats to great loss.

Jake, studying this situation of reefs, had devised a plan for us to get our 5 foot keeled sailboat around in a fishhook shaped route, longer but safer, to get to the island where we hoped our family awaited. This took most of the day, and getting to the rendezvous in the early afternoon we found that they were there. That was quite the feat in our view for them to handle the boat, the reefs, the islands, and find the right place. We all arrived there within 4 hours of each other.

Jake parted company with Bes at that point, and Sandra took his place as a one-woman crew for the remainder of the 2000-mile sail to New Orleans. Sandra and I departed there after a week on the last leg which was to take us another 1400 miles plus. Our oldest son, James Hammond Eve IV, arrived and spent a week after which they all motorboated out and flew home. Sandra and I as it turned out, would sail for 4 more weeks getting back to New Orleans.

From the island retreat, as the crow flies, Sandra and I would have about a 250 mile trip to Miami. Sailing in the Atlantic, east of the Abacos, we were trolling as usual, with a silver spoon and big game fishing rig, when a dorado hit, about 4 feet long, close to 100 yards behind the boat. This started a struggle that I was sure would wind up with the fish still in the water, but by and by we got him closes and closer. This fish is like a neon light flashing different colors through the clear cobalt water, a phenomenon that is mesmerizing. Getting him worn out so the fight was depleted, he came to be on his side hardly moving. I got a gaff into him, lifted him aboard into the cockpit, and stretched him out on the bottom, which he pretty well filled up. It appeared that he was dead, and that was good news. But after a few minutes he recovered and started framming and flopping and thrashing and flinging blood in all directions. Eventually I got him butchered and into the freezer, to feed us for weeks to come. The Abaco island was scrub bush, no sign of civilization. Around the tip and back up north a bit we entered a lagoon with clear water down to 30 feet, everything visible, sponges, conchs, fish. Spent the night there, then on west the next day.

This took us past the Berry Islands, aimed for Bimini. This was a long leg, water about 20 feet deep or less. Along the way the battery bank shorted out. The batteries started melting from the charge that the engine put out when the engine was running. This was out of sight so I did not know what was going on. Eventually we got into Bimini, middle of the night. I could not find the entry to the little harbor there, and about that time discovered that our batteries were burned up and melted in a big running mess and we had no way to start the engine. So, if we had gotten into the harbor, we most likely would have to have been towed out to deep water. As it was, we anchored in about 30 feet of water in the open ocean west of Bimini, and departed under sail only the next day, headed for Miami and the customs and immigration checkin.

Entering Miami from the ocean is through a long canal called Government Cut. There is a heavy traffic in cruise ships, lunatics shooting around like bullets on jet skis, and what is probably drug sales enabled cigarette boats with bikini whatzits and their young men racing throughout without heed to anyone. The route takes you right into a congested area of marinas, with a tide flowing through, where one has to go in and out of narrow passages under bridges to get to a dock to disembark and get a taxi to get to customs wherein you tell them you did not bring any stuff or people from somewhere else with you.

You are supposed to check in immediately come hell or dead batteries. But, if you don't tell them you have arrived, what then. No one could manage to sail a big sailboat in these currents round and about the cramped marina, docking and getting it secured. I just could not get situated to be able to comply with the checkin, so we sailed on south till a bay opened up, where we edged over toward shore where cars were driving on paved roads, and anchored.

We had a folding hand truck on the boat. I put that in the dinghy and started rowing to find batteries. Those in Bes were 2 volt golf cart batteries. I intended to replace them with 12 volt. Got to shore, dragged the dinghy up

87

on the riprap rocks, got the handtruck and started wheeling it down the road. Eventually I came to a convenience store, no other store of any kind anywhere, went in there and found two big 12 volt batteries, which were the only batteries they had. Got them, backtracked, took a day getting it all working again. I opted not to go back north for the customs fake process. If they want to catch someone with an offense, they need to intercept the boat as it comes in; not tell them to dock, get a cab, go to their office, and explain what illegal drugs and stowaway illegals they are bringing to the USA.

We could have sailed around Florida and come ashore as a first contact with customs at the Ft. Myers office. So I took the position that we were just arriving and set off to do that.

First stop was Dinner Key, where the Miami police station is, what you see in the movies, especially Miami Vice, glass, beautiful building and site, hard to imagine this as the police station.

From there on south then west down the outside of the keys was a dull slog, no beach, scrub bush on land, for the most part. About half way down, on the eastern keys, maps show coral reefs offshore a few hundred yards, various coral reef state parks. People would race up to us in their power boats looking for the reefs, not knowing they were underwater and visible only if you went underwater. Key Largo had an interior lake accessible by a long narrow waterway which we motored up for a one-night rest. Much to the dismay of the few speedboats and cigarette boats that came up behind us, they had to just follow along, no space to get past.

Most of this leg was, no wind in the morning, picking up to 2 knots midday, a bit better in the afternoons. There was never a time on this leg when we made good time except for one storm which really sped things up. Finally, we came up on Marathon key, tried to get in there, veered about 2 inches off the channel, ran aground, got off, hell with this, went out and anchored in the ocean. A bit further south from Marathon is a waterway that allows one to pass into Florida Bay without having to go around Key West. Miami to Key

West is about 150 miles. Florida Bay was a pleasant interlude from the stresses of the past week. Sailing was easy, waves moderate, wind direction beneficial, lots of floats for stone crab traps everywhere.

The next big stressor was trying to deal with customs and immigration again. I had looked up the next best checkin point and thought it to be Port Everglades, without information on where Port Everglades was. I was vaguely familiar with Everglades City and thought, mistakenly, that was the right spot. Somewhere between when I was in high school about 1958 and the present, someone decided to call Fort Lauderdale Port Everglades, or so it appeared to me, a touristy thing I suppose. Getting to Everglades city in our boat was nearly impossible with a 5 foot keel. It is a 2 mile long ditch in the mangroves, some underwater logs here and there. But, we kept on, bumping and grounding and finally got to the end, where people stared at us as if we had lost our minds. I got Customs on the marine channel and told them where we were and that we were ready to check in.

For starters, they were highly pissed, told us to rent a car and drive it to their office in Ft. Myers and present ourselves to them under threat of being arrested. I told them we were pretty much beyond the boundary of civilization and no rental car was anywhere near this part of Florida. They never relented on this so we just pulled the anchor and motored back out into the ocean on the west side of Florida and proceeded north to Ft. Myers. Along the way we anchored at Marco Island where I contacted customs again. Got the same guy as before, who told me we were in deep you know what and that he had been severely reprimanded for how he had handled this mess and I had to get a rental car in Marco and head immediately for Ft. Myers and their office. I told him that we were anchored out in the water and by time I got somewhere to leave the boat and get a car we could have sailed to Ft Myers and it just made no sense so we would continue and contact them again from Ft. Myers.

We got into a marina at Ft. Myers, called customs, who said we had to report to the Ft. Myers airport, everyone on board to be present. I called a friend who lived there, Ray Schwartz. Ray left a party to come deal with this. Pick us up, take us to the airport customs office, stick with us through the interrogation or arrest or whatever they were to come up with, and take us back to the boat when and if we were cleared. Got to the right place, customs as nice as could be, like no unpleasantness had ever happened. No one mentioned the hostilities that had taken place over the previous two days nor the ridiculous demands made of us.

Back at sea again, we proceeded north uneventfully to Tampa Bay where we experienced a severe electrical storm, lightning and thunder at deafening levels. A sailboat is supposed to have a cone of protection if the rigging is grounded so lightning avoids or does no damage. None hit us. I have never been hit while on the boat. But, Armordillo was hit once and Bes twice. Both times exploded the lights and antenna at the top of the mast and did no further damage.

There are shoals along the coastline, here and there all along the Florida west coast and panhandle and beyond on the route to New Orleans. You can be many miles offshore, somewhere between 5 and 10 miles, and suddenly the water gets a bright green from light reflecting off the shallow sand bottom and you had best attend to it.

We pulled in for a night at Tarpon Springs. Niece and husband, Moira and Ralph Hinson, brought us some groceries from Tampa, managed to find us at a public dock. We had been cooked in that boat with the excessive heat ever since we got down to mid Florida latitudes, worn out from the heat. It was something of a turning point for me, just not wanting any more of the stifling heat.

From there on to New Orleans was unremarkable as for sailing, except for running aground a couple of times, which is unremarkable. The coast had been devastated by Katrina. Passing west offshore from Mississippi, close enough to see what was on shore, there was nothing on shore. Houses, stores, gone. No people, no cars, no lights at night, no boats. Midday one day I was asleep in the cabin, Sandra was doing the sailing, on a reach down the coast, which was pleasant with nice winds, when we realized a coast guard boat had started shadowing us, about 100 yards behind and off the port quarter. Sandra had on shorts and a white blouse with lace, just like she emerged from a fashion show. I wondered what they wondered about that. Was she alone? What could anyone possibly be doing out here, no infrastructure, where could she be going. Eventually they slowed down, got further away, and we lost track of them.

Dolphins would come racing toward the boat like a pack of friendly dogs coming home, jumping and frolicking, headed for the bow and riding the pressure wave under water and popping up right under the bowsprit. Sandra would race up and lie down on the bow right above them, at which point some would flip water in her face.

Getting back into Louisiana waters, after hand steering this boat for 2000 miles, we came to docks gone, broken pilings, stubs, all that was remaining, could not get the boat right up to our bulkhead for all the rubble. A neighbor saw us arriving by sail after having seen us drive off by car and truck about two months earlier. The yard was covered with rubble from other docks that had piled up on our yard, a pile of lumber about 6 feet deep. Roger got a board and put it out to the edge of the boat so we had a gangplank to get off the boat. From then on it was several years trying to get our house back together and fight the insurance company, flood and hazard, with Allstate, which did not go well.

Having been reconsidering whether dealing with the heat and tribulations of long-distance sailing in the South was right for us as we got older, and having Bes sit at the dock in New Orleans hardly used any more, we decided we had had enough of it and put her up for sale. She stayed on the market for 5 years. Lots of people came out for sailing lessons. I put it this way because they had a big dream that involved sailing this type of boat on the ocean, but had no idea what it involved nor how to handle her. Some simple thing like standing up in the cockpit on a run when the boat was about to gybe and nor realizing that someone could be killed when the boom swept across the cockpit, identified their readiness, which was not ready. Several brought their little dogs along.

February 16, 2011, finally concluded the sale effort in a very peculiar way. I had been corresponding with Phil, from Canada, who wanted to inspect Bes as part of a trip via New Orleans, to Guatemala. For more than a month, the Phil aspect matured, and he was going to take a train from Canada to New Orleans. We went back and forth about all that, and it was finally agreed that after he got to New Orleans, on Saturday February 12, he would take the city bus to the most distant point in this direction, which would be the Viet village 7 miles west of here, and I would pick him up at 10:20 am and bring him out for inspection, and take him back.

Several days prior to this, Dr. P showed up in the inbox, saying he wanted to take a look, was coming in to Pensacola on Sunday, leaving Tue, had a meeting Mon, was moving to Pensacola. When could he get over here, 6 hour round trip, he asked? Timing did not seem favorable, so it was up in the air, but he was interested.

Back and forth with Dr. P about how this could work, not getting much of anywhere with it, and I told him about Phil coming on Saturday.

Meantime, snow in the north interfered with the train, which finally broke down in Chicago and Phil, off the train in a hotel waiting for trip to resume, said, from Chicago, he could not get here Sat, so we set same schedule for Sun.

I told Dr. P that Phil was coming Sunday and maybe Dr. P, if he did not mind, could come at the same time. Talked to Doc till the phone surely was ready to expire from dead battery. Doc finally said he wanted to buy the boat before Phil could show up and buy it. He wanted to send a deposit by paypal, how much did I want, or mail a check, or bring a check with him to Pensacola. He knew he was putting me in an awful position, but he wanted the boat. I told him 10%, but reminded him that we had not determined a sale price. I said I had it advertised on Craigslist and was that an acceptable price? He said it was. He was set to fly out next day, and as I was not all that familiar with paypal, I said to bring it with him. He said he was worried about hull condition, rudder condition, and deck condition, and wanted the sale contingent on a certified survey that addressed these points. No way to get this done in a short timeframe, complete unknown, and aggravation of what a surveyor may do, could derail the whole thing for no legitimate reason. Was she sold, or not, who knew, not me? Drank way too much rum that night.

Meantime, Phil had arrived in New Orleans on Sat and said by email he would be at the Viet village on Sunday as agreed. I sent him an email, as this is how we had been corresponding, telling him Bes was sold and pickup cancelled, in different words than that.

Meantime, Patrick had a 4pm tue departure flight, wanted to be back to kids about noon, so decided to come out here departing Pensacola at 3:30 am for inspection.

So, this was Sun, I think, hiatus till Patrick arrived at 7am on tuesday, no time to deal with survey and conditions on hull etc, wondering what to do. As Doc's concerns, had he known more about it, would have been known to be unmerited, I had no enthusiasm for lending credence or time to these concerns, did not know how long this could drag out, what the outcome would be. I decided to try to explain to him that his worries were misplaced, hence the fin keel vs full keel piece I copied you on.

Also, he was leery of propane, thought the boat was in danger of blowing up, did not want the refrigeration, he thought, and wanted to take out the toilet and use a bucket. These things he just saw as modifications he would make after he became owner, not a contingency for the sale.

So, my email to Phil said it was sold even though i was not sure that was true, and said my pickup of him was off, this sent on Saturday. Now waiting for Doc to show up Tue am wondering how that would turn out, now said the boat was off the market. Took the yankee off and washed it, a major operation that took probably 4 hours. Sunday and Monday rolled around as I was moving all the sail stuff out of the attic and Sandra and I were washing and organizing, and phone rang Sunday and Phil wondered where I was, he was in Viet village waiting for me. I explained that the boat was sold and that I had sent him an email. He was very upbeat and mature about all this, said he wished he had read his emails, congrats on selling the boat, and he thought he would just go to a Viet restaurant now that he was out here, then back to NO then to Ft. Lauderdale then to Guatemala.

This leaves us getting ready for Doc's visit. Tue was overcast and dark, cold, boat wet from dew, so I lit the propane inside, and decided to turn on all the nav lights, except, that the masthead tricolor, the requirement for night sailing, had never come on since we bought the boat, so I knew that would be a deficiency. Flipped all the switches, went out to check, and every nav light was on, including the tricolor. I have no explanation for that, maybe I never found the right switch or combination. Will check on it later to try to figure it out, but mind you, I am not complaining.

Doc showed up on time, went over the boat in excruciating detail, found things to ask about that I had never seen, like what is this, where does that go and so on. took the dinghy and went around the outside in such detail that he found a ding that was 1/2 in wide on the side, painted over, I thought invisible, he put his finger on it and asked about it.

I explained the propane, propane locker, gas detection, refrigeration, amp draw, uses, how much propane could be stored, i.e., a years' worth or more is now on board. It got on to around noon, and he sat down and wrote me out a check for the whole amount. All the conditions gone like a wisp of fog in the sunshine.

You have seen from other emails where this has gone since.

So, you see, nothing worth mentioning at all, so much for your assertion that there is always a story.

Love Dad
From: Jacob Eve
Subject: story, what story?
Date: Wednesday, February 16, 2011, 12:35 PM

I read this twice, still had difficulty coming to terms with it, got out a notepad and made charts and graphs. (this, I am not kidding). After reading it the first time, was left with the impression that all involved parties were either insane, partially insane, or demonstrated ever so slightly insane behavior, but had to chart it to confirm.

Let's start with Phil. He's from Canada coming to New Orleans on his way to Guatemala, by train. Something wrong from the start here. Who travels such distances by train? Is this possible? How could anyone set up a visit and never have made a phone call, all done on email. Phil is an odd character right off the bat. 5 insanity points awarded.

Then we have Doc. First, how can two people be arriving to look at Bes on the same day or within 2 days of each other when Bes has been for sale for 5 years? And it comes down to this? Doc asks how long is the round trip between Pensacola and NO. First indication he has some issues. 2 insanity points right off the bat. MapQuest anyone??? On Sunday, Doc learns Phil is coming to look at boat and sight unseen, decides to buy boat. Doc is now insane. 100 insanity points for Doc.

Then Doc wants to use Paypal but doesn't know how. 5 more points. Then wants a full boat survey. Ok, take away a few insanity points. Then he wants to take out the toilet and use a bucket. Now Doc is in the fully insane category--I would think all this is going the way of a swamp land sale. 50 more insanity points for Doc.

Meanwhile, Phil manages to take trains from Canada to New Orleans and then find out which bus to take to Viet village, thus losing at least two insanity points. But Phil doesn't call until he is at Veit village, waiting on Dad, thus gaining back 10 insanity points.

Phil calls Dad. Phil is 10 minutes away. Dad has never seen Doc. Doc has already amassed so many insanity points he is now rated as fully insane. Allegedly, Doc is going to show up on Tuesday. Dad tells Phil the boat is already sold. Dad has no deposit and has no idea whether Doc will show or not. Phil is 10 minutes away. Phil may buy boat. Phil has gone way out of his way and demonstrated some resolve in getting to Viet village. Dad gets 10 insanity points for telling Phil boat is sold.

Doc does, in fact, show on Tuesday, writes check for boat on the spot. Doc won't pick up boat until much later. Dad could sell boat to someone else, after depositing check--not that he would ever do that, but Doc gets a few more insanity points.

I am still very nervous about all of this. Is the check real? Will it fund? Will Doc later decide he doesn't want boat, no contract signed, then sue to get money back? Doc isn't normal, but then again, neither is Phil. Maybe no Westsail boat owner is normal???

And there's no story here? Jake

CHAPTER 18

BES MOVES ON

Bes, a Westsail 32, length overall of about 40 feet, built in 1976, named after the Egyptian goddess of pleasure, changed owners in February, 2011. The new owner, Dr. P., an MD, Family Practice, was moving to Pensacola, FL, and asked me to help get her over there and teach him how to sail a big boat along the way, and he wanted to do deep water as much as possible. He was a sailing instructor in college, so knew the basics of how a sailboat works.

April 5, 2011, we got started out from our residence in the far east part of New Orleans, on the high tide, the only way over the mud bar, in the late afternoon, Tuesday. Wind mild as we proceeded S through the Chef Pass, the two bridges, car and train, and into a bay called Lake Borgne, turned E, and slowly progressed till evening when we anchored in open water for the night.

Next day, Wednesday, wind really kicked up from the SE so we were obliged, as a sailboat won't go straight into the wind under sail, to proceed along the coast into Mississippi waters, at which time the wind had gotten stronger. We came up behind Ship Island, about 15 miles off the MS coastline, and anchored in protected waters. Spent the next day working on the boat. Pat went up the mast using a climbing contrivance that clamps on to a taunt rope, and works by clamping and sliding, up or down, alternately, on the rope, hands then feet, hands then feet, etc, sort of like an inchworm climbs a rope. It appeared to be quite a struggle as I lay on my back on the deck below with belay rope in hand. He took down two dead bulbs and replaced another, checked 3 wires for power to try to figure out why the deck light did not work, replaced the deck light bulb, took some chaff protectors that had become trashed off the shrouds, and came down.

The area was teeming with dolphins, young and old, so the worst oil spill in US history, which was maybe 75 miles from here (this is a guess) did not do in the dolphins, as some had surmised.

Pat swam over to the beach and visited the fort while I caught up on essential learning, which was, what had happened to Sherlock Holmes in the adventure of the league of red headed gentlemen, on the Kindle, accompanied by some spirits, as is a naval custom, when at sea, reading about Sherlock Holmes.

Next day pulled anchor and went back a bit and rounded the W end of island, in the shipping fairway, which took us from about 20 foot depth to about 45 foot depth, and headed S, toward the Gulf, intending to go this next night inside the Chandeleur Islands. These islands were formed by the outflow of the Mississippi River, centuries ago when the river course was different. Flooding upstream at that time breached the natural berms many miles from the mouth, diverting the flow into the current channel, and abandoning sedimentation of this area we now approached. Over time, the land sank by natural processes, leaving this crescent shaped island, named after a chandelier, as it somewhat resembles a string of pearls from the air. So, our goal was to have one more sheltered anchorage before the open waters of the Gulf of Mexico (GOM), or gulf.

Soon after getting into this shipping channel, I put out a deep-sea fishing rig with an artificial squid and very heavy line, trailing behind the boat, rod secured in a rod holder on the stern pulpit. About 15 minutes after this, something hit, like the proverbial freight train. There were hundreds of yards of line on this huge reel, and the fish stripped most of it out in short order, and the end was approaching, where the fish would break the line and that would be the end of catching that fish. We turned the boat around and started chasing the fish, reeling in trying to recover line, chasing round and round back and forth, reeling in as best we could, Pat doing most of the reeling in.

Once we recovered enough line, wound back on the reel so if the fish made another run the drag gearing in the reel would slow him down and tire him out, theoretically, we would try to resume our direction to the Chandeleur Islands, dragging the fish, so we thought, wearing him down some more, so we thought, so it had gone in all instances in the past. Eventually we would have him near the boat worn out and floating on his side, at which time we could put a definite end to the drama.

The only position of boat and fish where we could put the rod in the rod holder was when the fish was behind the boat, and we were going forward, and the fish was not making a run to go under the boat. As this developed, we were hardly ever in that position.

So, I drove the boat, and Pat reeled whenever he could, and had to position himself here and there on the boat as we tried to keep the fish away from the boat till he (the fish) tired out. In so doing, the butt of the rod was digging into various parts of the rod holder, that would be Pat, into stomach, inner thighs. He got some damaged blood vessels and other injuries from this, because the fish was, it turned out, more powerful than we were.

This struggle continued into the day, in the end lasting for 5 ½ hours and we never saw the fish. At times we thought he was wearing down, and may surface near the boat, and I was standing by to gaff him, but we never raised him into sight. We covered a distance of 25 miles fighting this fish, a track on the GPS suggestive of a wandering drunk, a situation we were becoming desirous of.

We succeeded in dragging, we thought, him toward the Islands where the water was shallower, hoping this would give us some advantage in getting him up from the depths where maybe we could pull him in. We thought he was done for at this point. Couldn't have been more wrong. He seemed to wake up from a light sleep, which may have been a fact as in the end we are not sure he was fully aware that we had him hooked, made a run that stripped out all the line again, the most powerful run of the day, turned around and headed for the boat faster than we could retreat, went under the boat, popped the line, and all we could think of was a religious statement, THANK GOD.

Because of this, we entered the area of the Northern Chandeleurs half a day behind schedule. Most people think Katrina eliminated these islands and wanted a report, back in my neighborhood, so we were interested in seeing what happened. Well, lighthouse on N end of island was gone without a trace, and the island, which had been miles long, was broken into parts, with a separated part on the end where the light house had been. I doubt that the end was where it used to be either. But, though reduced, and not as high, and not as many dunes, it was still there, along the old trace.

We proceeded in the sound behind it still headed for GOM deep water, when a fog bank rolled in and we could not see 50 yards. It became apparent that there was some oil industry stuff going on based on big boat traffic passing near us in the fog, and we had seen some large block shaped structure on the horizon, like a motel on a barge, so we thought the traffic; was related to their going to whatever that was. Not a rig or platform, something else. This caused us to edge up to shallower water, near grounding, a depth large commercial boats would shy away from. Spent the night in the fog, woke up in the fog, ate our Dinty Moore beef stew with dumplings following Sandra's technique of using the can for a pot, in the fog. Waited in the fog. And waited some more.

Finally got fed up with the stew and the fog and started moving slowly S. This eventually got us to the S end of the chain where it turned West, a direction we did not want to go, and as it was about 3 pm, and we did not want to probe the shoals in the dark trying to get on the other side to deep water, we anchored. Beautiful protected waters, Chandelier Islands about a half mile off.

Next day, the Cape May Warbler visited. Hopped all around us, eating tiny creatures we could not see, in crevices, with its needle like beak. Pat tried to get it on his finger, but a couple inches away was all Mr. Warbler would put up with, so he would flit away a few inches. Mr. W went in the cabin but hunting was not as good, so it was back in the cockpit, all around us. Stayed with is at least an hour.

During this time, we were forced to go West along the shoals. Some islands that used to exist, Curfew island, maybe Freemason Island, were entirely gone, but shoals were left behind, the surf from the S winds pounding on them, and we could not get by. Kept going W, opposite the direction we needed to go to get to Pensacola.

I was beginning to wonder if we would ever get out of this box canyon. Nightmare scenario would be having to go back the way we came, all the way to Ship island to get out of this trap, and if that, I may as well take Pat back to New Orleans so he could catch the plane from there to go to his daughter Maggie's prom, and Bes would be back at our dock where this adventure started.

By and by we saw on the GPS a double line, and found it to be a submerged pipeline. Not knowing if we would hit it, but we had to cross it, we edged up and found it to be about 2 feet deeper than the surrounding seafloor. Bear in mind that we were in water generally 5 or 6 feet deep, the boat draws about 5 feet, so it is a tedious way to progress, and every few inches of depth is a big help. We started following the pipeline, staying right over it, and that went well, except we were again aimed at Galveston when we were trying to get to Pensacola. After about an hour of this I started trying to determine by advancing the GPS cartography on the screen, just where this pipeline went and if it ever turned south and went through the shoals we were trying to cross. It did, some 8 or 10 miles further west, leaving the question, could we follow it into deep water, or did it just rise up over shoals we could not cross.

Nothing to do but soldier on, verging on grounding continuously, or turn around completely and head back as mentioned before.

I put out the fake squid again, and another freight train hit it within minutes. By this time, I had tightened the drag to the point where it would seem sufficient to drag a log, and the line did not break in my testing of it on the boat, so we figured we could just drag the hell, or health, out of any monster that chose to get on. So, this became a contest between BES, the 20,000-pound boat, and Perkins, the 40 hp diesel moving Bes at the time, and the fish. Well, of the three, nothing yielded. Bes pulled the fish, which if possible, gave me the impression that it was even bigger than the first. The engine propelled Bes. The fish dragged like a log, a solid hard pull that was relentless and way beyond the power of the reel to overcome.

Mr. Fish would veer off with power to port, then same to starboard, an unyielding and continuing hard pull. We decided we would just drag Mr. Fish to Pensacola, if we could ever get out of this box canyon, and maybe beach him and at that point maybe we would have the upper hand with him on land. So, all parties were stalemated, as we proceeded in the opposite direction from our destination, over the pipeline, behind the shoal, pulling Mr. Fish.

Then, with no fanfare, Mr. Fish got off. Thank God.

Approaching the point where the pipeline angled for deeper water, we started probing the shoal again and eventually passed over with several inches' clearance under the keel. The depth did not increase for a long time, maybe a half mile, so we were still in danger of running aground during that time, but finally it got to 7 feet, and compared to what we had been through, that was a blessing.

Got turned a bit toward the SE, in deep water, headed out for the depths that Pat wanted experience in, got up the main with one reef, the staysail, and the yankee, and while this was going on, Pat on the cabin top reefing the main, these tan blobs, about 18-24 inches wide, a bit longer, by the hundreds, started showing up one to two feet under the surface of the beautifully tinted green water. I was a bit distracted from paying close attention to that while we were attending to getting under way with the sails, so it was not clear just what this stuff was. For a while I thought it was a huge flotilla of the parachute shaped jellyfish, but finally realized that a stingray migration was passing right under the boat. I had seen some pictures of this phenomenon taken from the air, and there would be thousands, so, I presume we were in the midst of thousands.

This put us on a 24/7 course in deep water, for deeper water, and at this time we started losing track of what day it was. We had strong winds driving us East all day, all night, all day, it becomes a blur as to days. Events are easier to chronicle.

During this long stretch, Pat started working with lashing the tiller so as to give some relief for the helmsman from the incessant tendency of the boat to turn into the wind, a tendency that is desirable in the sense that if the tiller is left untended, the boat turns into the wind and stops moving forward. He got this down to a science and we were continually appreciative of the self-correcting balancing act the boat assumed under these conditions, Mr. Lash at the tiller, tireless, always adjusting to wind shifts. Much to Pat's chagrin, he discovered that Mr. Lash did a better job than he himself did. But, Mr. Lash does not know everything. If the wind dropped and boat speed fell off, ie, turned away from her course so as to get sideways to the wind, Mr. Lash did not know what to do and Mr. Pat had to fix it.

Wind behind the boat, Mr. Lash at a complete loss, so Mr. Pat was needed again, and felt somewhat better about himself. Going to windward, however, Mr. Lash beat Mr. Pat in paying attention to little wind shifts.

Through the day it was just plain sailing in good conditions and beautiful surroundings. Rigs and platforms would be visible in the distance, all with horns blowing at intervals like oceanic vessels on the move. They would rise up in

103

the distance as the curvature of the earth and our progress revealed them, and disappear in our wake in the same manner. As night and full darkness came on, their lights would then become the only thing visible, many with a multitude of lights. The underside of these structures is about 50-60 feet or more above the sea surface, and they may be another 75 feet or so high extending above that. So, they were way up there, but they would still rise up over the horizon as we approached and drop from sight as we left them behind.

We had had enough of the trolling business so did not pick it up again till quite close to landfall approaching Pensacola. Somewhere in here we discovered that a seam at the top of the mainsail had parted, threads rotted, and the only thing holding the leach of the sail together was a basting tape. We sailed on with a split sail aloft.

So, to recap the events in order, from Mr. Warbler on, we have second big fish, crossing the shoals, entering the deeper water, the stingray migration, the rising and falling of the offshore rigs and platforms, day into night into day, on the move, then come the Portuguese Man-of-Wars.

This thing is a beautiful, or hideous, scary, sort of obscene, colonial animal that is passively predatory, the way a flycatcher plant is passively predatory, made of jelly. This particular one has brilliant colors, vivid glowing purple, blue, violent, magenta, within the generally clear material of its body. The oddest thing about it, never mind, it is all odd, is that it has a sail. It also has a waterline, like a sailboat. Below the waterline are the orderly hubs of tentacles that house nematocysts that consist of a coiled spring, a poison dart, and a trigger, a completely independent mechanism held in place by strands of jelly tissue, ready to fire when touched by anything.

Above the waterline are two bladders, one about 4 inches across on an average sized animal, and 6 to 10 inches long, filled with air I presume, rising up like a mound several inches above water. There is a second one, thin, under an inch thick, 6 or 8 inches long, attached to the top of the previous, sticking up to function as a sail, approaching a foot high for a large one. This is all tinted in neon colors visible from as much as a hundred yards, as they so sailing along, on a path not directed by any intelligence, just a factor of winds and currents. Tentacles are dangerous.

The nematocysts are still functional when separated from the host. Sometimes strong wave actions separate some of these cells or strands which then hit swimmers and discharge, leaving a mystified person with itches all over wondering what is happening.

Winds fell off and it became apparent that we were not going to sail to windward and reach a distant goal that Pat had set, somewhere off Naples FL, and we had better get on toward the harbor or Pat was going to be in trouble over the prom. This put us on a slow and sleepy course, sort of sloshing along, watching the Man-of-Wars sail by, headed for Pensacola Bay via McRee Inlet, which I have now decided needs the services of an exorcist.

Along in here, maybe 50 miles out from Pensacola Bay, a trio of bottle nosed dolphins showed up. Seeing them approach from a distance is comical once you understand what is going on. They have detected a boat they want to play with, and they hustle with all their considerable might and power to get to the bow of the boat in short order. They come on the run, so to speak, shoulder to shoulder, pounding through the water, surfacing and diving and casting spray in their haste to get to the boat, like a pack of friendly dogs coming to their master for a welcome home.

On reaching the boat they go immediately to the bow and start weaving back and forth, rubbing against each other occasionally, sometimes stopping all swimming motion entirely as they mysteriously move forward with no apparent effort, then they will turn upside down, zoom off in a flash, zoom back in, turn sideways, maybe flip a fluke at the person on the boat to splash them in the face, then go off laughing.

On we went, to McRee inlet. This is a narrow-shoaled passage through which, best as I can tell, all the tidal action of the huge Pensacola Bay, and long and

105

wide rivers upstream, pass. Sandra and I went through here coming from Bahamas, entering with an outgoing tide which was a torrent that pretty near brought the boat, which was under engine and sail, to a standstill, and rolled her over gunwale to gunwale at some point of turbulence midway through, where waves were jumping straight up toward heaven, a very odd situation.

SPat and I were approaching this place, studying it from a distance to try to see just where to go to avoid the shoals and get through. I pointed out to Pat that if you are going into a tricky situation, get the engine going and warmed up so you can get a boost of power if needed, but there was no reason at this point to think it would be needed. Following that rule, however, we got er warmed up and ready for a push.

During our approach, Pat got the impression that we were going to pass through the bright green breakers to the left, where it appeared to me that we needed to leave that whole turbulent mess off to port. But, none of this was clear from the distance we were observing, so we cautiously moved forward.

After we got a bit closer, I spotted some small barrel shaped channel markers off to starboard and told Pat to turn to starboard. This was going to take about a 90 degree turn to get us in position, but as Pat thought we were still going in through the breakers he gave just a suggestion of a turn in that direction. This bit of delay got us right in the breakers, sideways, being carried toward the beach. Water depth decreased from 13 to 12 then 10, and at that point I put the engine in full forward and got Pat oriented as to just how far back we had to turn to get out of this mess, and he responded immediately.

Next wave that passed under and left us in the trough dropped us down to a depth of 7 feet. In these conditions, if the boat hits bottom, it does not move out as the wave recedes, then the next wave picks it up and pushes it further up the beach, and the next does the same and it winds up on its side stranded on the beach. That is the situation we narrowly averted.

We finally got in position to enter the inlet under motor and sail and went on in, then into a lagoon off to port. This is a T shaped situation, big lagoon behind dunes to the left, and widening river to right which shortly becomes Pensacola Bay. Next day we would cross the landward side of the inlet and go into Pensacola Bay and thence to the marina where Pat had arranged a haulout.

This lagoon, called Big Lagoon, was a beautiful place, same place Sandra and I stayed when we came this way. Winds became very strong from the South, which was off the Gulf, so we moved up fairly close to the protective dunes which ran along the beach, anchoring just far enough out so if the wind changed during the night, we would still be clear of being aground.

The Blue Angels started a performance for hours right over our heads. I don't know how they knew we were coming. This went on till late afternoon. Then we had our usual meal of filet mignon, or grilled salmon, and a happy hour, and went to sleep.

Wind did change during the night, becoming a strong wind from the North, or landward side at this point. We were anchored in the SE part of the lagoon, which means the wind was blowing us toward the dunes that were right behind us, and the end of the lagoon was just a bit off to our starboard side as Bes was facing North.

This is normally not a problem, as you just start the engine, motor forward till over the anchor, get the anchor in, motor forward some more, get the sails all up, going straight into the wind, and at that point you can turn the boat about 45 degrees or so to one side or the other and get the sails in operation and move forward without the engine. The engine solves the problem of the wind blowing the boat backward into the dunes behind before the sails can get her moving forward, and gets you over the anchor so you can get that in and get under way by sail. And, if there were plenty of room behind the boat, the engine would be unneeded cause the boat could be blown backward without consequence after the anchor was pulled, and the room needed to get moving under sail would be there. But the engine would not start.

This left us under anchor, anchor dug in, bow into the wind, shallow water near on the starboard side and right behind the boat, and no engine to get us moving right out of there. We were faced with getting the anchor in, the sails up, getting blown backward and to one side or the other until we could get the boat moving forward under sail. Question at this point, how to do this and can we get her going forward quick enough.

While we were thinking this over, I noticed that the boat would go back and forth on the anchor, sort of tacking in place. We did not want to head off to starboard as the shallow water was much closer on that side, so we resolved to winch the boat forward till she was right over the anchor, but still held in place, and when she veered off to port in this going back and forth mode she had been in, we would, all in a flash, pop out the anchor and deploy the foresail (yankee as it is called) and sail right out of there on starboard tack, away from the shoals behind and to our right.

But, pulled up short on the anchor, she stopped going back and forth, and instead adopted this stubborn posture that would put her on port tack headed for the closer shallow water. Blue Angels realized we were still there and kept at it all day again.

Our situation was not solving itself, and as it was 3pm at this point, and we were supposed to be at a haulout at 8am next day some distance away at a marina off Pensacola Bay, and we had been messing with the engine all day also, and had gotten it to where it ran at a slow idle when at full throttle and shut off if we put it in gear, and that it was unlikely to improve, and since we were getting tired of and fed up with this situation, we decided to go for it and do the best we could. Got the mainsail up, yankee ready to deploy, popped the anchor but left it dangling, gave it a try, did not get enough speed, dropped the anchor again even in a worse situation as we lost ground, headed off on the tack we were trying to avoid.

Gave it another go, same procedure, more risk, got up some speed, tacked, and we were out of the trap and headed for the larger part of the lagoon. Next trial, as the wind dropped, was crossing the landward side of McRee Inlet, without power, without adequate wind, and without being carried by the currents back out into the gulf. We readied the anchor, which we were going to drop if the tides got ahold of us, and proceeded lamely. At this point I decided to try to start the engine with it in gear, in forward, and she fired up, turning so slowly you could look in the water and pick any propeller blade you wanted and watch it go round and round. The engine was turning so slowly it seemed impossible that it could keep running, but it did. This gave us propulsion of between a half mile and one mile an hour and the meager wind at this point gave us about the same, so we proceeded at about a mile and hour. Tide was about at a standstill so we got past McRee inlet into Pensacola bay, about a mile, when the tide turned against us and brought us to a near standstill, not much different than when we were moving.

Next issue, assuming the wind would ever blow and we could get moving again, and at this point we were thinking it might take all night to get to this marina,we discovered that the GPS mapping around Pensacola Bay to the north was undeveloped. The small river we were supposed to go up was not on the map and we did not know where it was. Pat had a city map, and we could find the marina on that map, but we could not find our current position on the city map. To sum this up, with the two maps, the GPS on the screen and the paper map in Pats hands, we could not find the position of both ourselves and the marina on either of the two maps. Pat had a big paper map of Pensacola Bay, but we could not find where the marina was on this one either. He called the marina and no one there could tell him how to get there by water from McRee inlet, which was right behind us.

Thinking this mess over, I realized that the only time I had seen all this stuff on one map was a google map back at home, so I asked Pat if he could get google on his phone. He said he could, called up google maps, got the marina location plotted on the tiny screen on the phone, but the river was so small we

109

could not find it on the phone screen, so what we had was a marina location that appeared inland somewhere with no attached waterway to reach it.

Wind picked up and we just aimed Bes at the shoreline out from where the X on the cell phone said the marina was. Could see nothing there that looked like an entry inland. Proceeded anyway, engine still cranking away and turning prop about as fast as someone pedals a bicycle, but every little bit counts, and we ran aground.

Going this slow it was not a hard grounding, so we got the foresail square to the wind and turned Bes around the other way, pivoting on the aft end of the keel. Propulsion was so weak by wind and engine at this point that we periodically lost steerage. We struggled around in this vicinity, looking at the phone, barely clearing the bottom as we moved about in the boat, and finally saw some larger boats coming in. They just went at the shoreline and disappeared, so there had to be an entry even though we could not see it.

We also discovered a channel, very narrow, some distance away and that was the only way to get in. We got over there, had to tack in with yankee, backwinding at every tack, getting only a short distance per tack, but finally got into more confined waters between docks, houses, boats, restaurants, etc., and brought in the sails and moved forward at a half knot under the engine only. We entertained every person in sight for quite a while with all this. They stopped what they were doing and stared. Stopped chewing the food in their mouths and stared. We are surely famous now. But they don't know who we were. Got to the marina about dark, coasted up to the entry to the travel lift and the engine ran no more. Would not start again, even the loping version of running any more.

A diesel engine has no spark plugs. A gas heats up on compression, so in a diesel, it is a high compression engine that explodes the fuel vapor by compression and heat. If the major parts of such an engine, rings, pistons, cylinders, are not in excellent condition, compression will be lost, the fuel vapor will not be heated sufficiently by compression to explode, therefore the engine won't run. The situation thus is that the engine block, the major parts that would be a big problem to fix, are in good shape. It seems to be a fuel supply problem, something outside the big block of iron and steel that comprises the bulk of the engine.

We proceeded, stared at by one and all, at a snail's pace, up this narrow passage between all these high end fancy boats and houses and so on. It is so slow, it is more like waiting, not moving, like sitting at a bus stop, waiting. At this point I had had about four Cuba Libres, and Pat had taken a tithe of each, even though he does not drink normally, and this being such a religious experience, he took a double tithe at least twice. As the day turned into night, we finally got to the marina, found a sign that said Pensacola Shipyard Marina, so we finally were sure, for the first time since all this started this day, that we were in the right place.

We got Bes turned around by hand, backed up ready for liftout, plugging the travellift approach heedless of what their plans of the morning might be, went swimming, cooked a couple of filet mignons, and that was it for the day.

Next day marina was pissed that we plugged up the chute, but went ahead and hauled Bes out. Sandra the speed demon had departed Waycross GA that morning to come get us. April 14, she showed up at the marina 10 minutes early and picked me up and took Pat to the airport.

Bes is now in capable hands, ready to be doctored and taken on trips and to entertain young and old alike, venturing out of Pensacola, Florida, same name, BES, new port of call.

April 15, 2011, New Orleans, Louisiana

CHAPTER 19

KATRiNA

Katrina killed 1,833 people, hurricane waters came 6 to 12 miles inland, property damage amounted to 125 billion dollars, and there were more than 50 breaches in the New Orleans levee system (Wikipedia)

My timespan for this book covers from about 1998 to 2018, obviously including one of the worst hurricane disasters in US history. But I dreaded getting into the subject for its sheer size. Worried about this for weeks, what could possibly be new in any narration of this well-publicized catastrophe, for it is all on the internet if one wants to do the time. There is a Katrina story from high altitude, but there are hundreds of thousands of Katrina stories from ground level. All these ground level stories have a commonality—displacement, loss of contact, uncertainty, hunger, worry, financial losses including devastation, sickness, injury, and sometimes death. So, I am going for a ground level commentary, the little things and struggles within the larger struggle, such as the loss of infrastructure for many miles in all directions.

Katrina went right over our house. The aftermath was, all docks, pilings, decks, stairs, railings on the outside of the house were destroyed, piled in a huge rubble pile between our house and the one to the north, a distance of about 40 feet. In this pile were the remains of other docks, several boats including one shrimp boat, a concrete alligator that weighed about 50 pounds, personal items from other people's houses, including adult and children's clothing, books, small items like vases and utensils, roofing shingles, glass, staircases, trucks, air compressor, generator.

All garage doors, other doors, windows on our lower lever were out. Mud 6 inches to a foot deep covered everything inside and outside of the house. Storm waters had gotten to our second level, bringing down the ceilings of the lower level, including all the fiberglass insulation. All the cabinets, furniture, tools on the lower level had been broken loose, broken apart, sloshed around with the mud and fiberglass as if in a washing machine. This left a mass of sludge and detritus knee deep throughout the lower level. The shingles and tarpaper were gone from the west slopes of the roof, bringing rainwater onto the ceiling on the top floor. Other parts of the roof were missing shingles in a scattered manner. Most of the siding and much soffit was gone. Many of the seals in the windows on the second and third floors were breached.

One of the major columns on the front porch second floor as well as the entire plantation style sweeping front staircase had been knocked out by a 60 foot derelict steel shrimp boat that moved through the neighborhood like a giant wrecking ball. The boat took out the entire outer wall second and third stories of my neighbor's house. I had a Ford crew cab in the driveway. That was moved about 20 feet, turned parallel to the street, and crushed as the shrimp boat passed over it. On the front seat of this truck was an air compressor that had been in the garage, somehow crashed through the windshield before the boat collapsed the roof of the truck. It took years to get the house back together, strung out by incessant struggles with the insurance company. Those instrumental in getting this done include our three sons, James Hammond Eve, IV, and Jacob H. Eve; Guy and Elizabeth Thurmond; neighbors, especially John Burlett and his sons, the local firefighters (on their own time), Ritchie Hinderlighter; and our Chinese friends Frank Yam and John Kwong.

Residence of Hammond and Sandra Eve, Venetian Isles, New Orleans

Some houses disappeared entirely. Some were lifted off the foundation and deposited intact somewhere else. My neighbor across the street was blessed with two houses after the storm. The second was a full sized wooden house that was moved onto his dock, half hanging out over the water, dropped down over the pilings which stuck up about 6 feet above the dock and pinned the house there. The house stayed there for over a year.

All utilities were out—gas, water, power. Streets became canyons as debris was piled on both sides 6 feet or better deep. It closed the streets down to one lane in places.

The storm hit August 29. It was a long period of uncertainty before we got back on November 4, which was the earliest time the Allstate adjustor could meet us. Most of that interim we knew we had a roof, but we did not know if there were a house under it. The adjustor worked on our claim for about half a day and said he would send a report later, and that he represented both our flood and hazard insurance claims. A month or better passed and we were stunned to see that his total assessment came to under $30K. Shortly after that we hired a private assessor firm for what turned out to be $6,000.

115

In the end, after the private assessor had worked on our claim for months, proving losses which Allstate ignored, and after many other assessors came and went, with wildly varying assessments of loss, we had gotten some $30K probably, but were still short. The Road Home program came along, eventually got to us, and determined that we were undercompensated by tens of thousands of dollars, which they then granted to us.

There was much confusion among adjustors, both Allstate and the private firm, as to what flood insurance covered in this neighborhood. Turns out that a frequently ignored requirement that all houses built after a certain date must be raised, and many were out of compliance with this, were not covered as they thought. For us, very little was covered on the lower level by any insurance even though we had both flood and hazard.

We passed the winter in the house, no utilities. We dipped salt water from the canal, and daily Sandra drove 30 miles to a state park with a working faucet and filled 5 gallon containers with fresh water. We cooked with a propane hotplate. Food was being supplied to firefighters nearby. We came to be feeding as many as 9 people at times, some of them firefighters. Some of the excess food prepped for the firefighters was given to us. In one case this amounted to about 30 barbecued chickens, and we had no refrigeration. One of the shrimp boats was operational, giving us mounds of seafood beyond our ability to eat it all. Eventually the Red Cross showed up in white food service trucks. The volunteers started servicing this neighborhood with one hot meal per day. This had to be a major sacrifice for them as there were no accommodations anywhere near here. They had to get up in the wee hours, get the food cooked, the truck stocked, and drive for at least an hour. They always arrived in good spirits and provided however many meals we asked for. Eventually they started bringing ice, which improved our lives immensely, not only for the BBQ chickens, but for much needed relaxing libations.

There are several images burned in my brain from this time during the winter. We have a tower in this house. From that tower, no light not from the heavens was seen in any direction at night. This neighborhood has natural gas. Some of the gas lines were broken. For a week or so there were houses burning. Helicopters with massive water pouches hanging under were flying about like Pterodactyls dousing the flames. Cranes were operating resembling T rexes. Smoke and flames and imitations of prehistoric creatures looked so much like hell.

CHAPTER 20

LiTTLE THiNGS CAN GET YOU DOWN

"**W**hoever can be trusted with very little can also be trusted with much, and whoever is dishonest with very little will also be dishonest with much. (Luke 16:10 NIV Bible)

The Federal Emergency Management Agency (FEMA) has a task akin to conducting a war minus the projectiles. Every imaginable emergency must be anticipated and a plan developed for magnitude, supplies, logistics, near and long-term remedies. Since Michael Brown, things have improved muchly and it appears that a good job has been done and overall it is a competent agency. So, this one little anecdote is just that, but it is an illustration of how one guy can screw up a program that affects hundreds of families and there seems to be no recourse nor supervisory cognizance. The canal system in Venetian Isles, where I live, is obviously public and navigable waters. There are no private property keep out signs and many people from other areas routinely come through. Prior to Katrina, most of the canals were deeper than after, and consequentially, many canals became somewhat plugged at the mouth. After much tooing and froeing, a boatload of Coast Guard, one FEMA contractor, several others and I came to be running a side scan sonar in the canals to identify hurricane impacts that would be subject to remediation by FEMA.

I was on the boat because I had done all this previously, using fish finder sonar, and made maps of every canal as to depth about every 50 feet. As one example of where this went completely off the rails, we look at the canal I live on. An above ground swimming pool was situated beside the canal at the mouth before Katrina. The mouth of the canal was 6 to 8 feet deep, and out from my dock the canal was 8 feet deep. After Katrina, the mouth was 3 feet or less and off my dock was 5 feet. I had probed the mouth, walked on it, dug in it, pulled up debris from it, and found that the entire pool that had been on land had been mutilated and buried in the mud across the center of the mouth of the canal. As we entered the canal, the FEMA guy, taking notes of the depth, noted, "the controlling depth of this canal is 3 feet, so FEMA will not consider any impacts for remediation unless they are above the height of the entry, which is 3 feet. There to consider remediation of hurricane damage, this FEMA contractor used the Katrina damage itself to define the baseline, rather than use the pre-Katrina condition to define the remediation of the impacts.

We went round and round on this, because clearly the shallow depth at the mouth was a consequence of the storm, and the swimming pool was proof, but he was totally blind to any further comment or dissent regarding his finding. His repeated argument, or response, was "I have been doing this for many years and I know exactly what I am doing, subject closed." This affected detrimentally every canal in the community and contributed to loss of value and utility of all homeowners.

This city is a huge tourist attraction. Tens of thousands of people come here in swarms for many occasions, holidays, conferences, sports events. The number of fines levied against these people is stunning. The stupidity of the fines is stunning in many cases. They will ticket you for parking on a sidewalk even if there is no sidewalk. If you bring a car, or rent one, chances are about a hundred percent that you will get a ticket and possibly get it impounded. Even with the best of intentions, it is very difficult to figure out what you must do with your car. My friend's car got stolen. It was reported to the police. During that time, it was used by the thief and got 3 parking tickets. He found his car, got taken to court for the tickets, and had to pay all fines for the time it was stolen. This highlights the fact that the license plates on ticketed cars were not run through the stolen car list. My neighbors' truck was stolen from his driveway. It was reported stolen. It had a little blue triangle on the bumper signifying this neighborhood. Cops saw it in the French Quarter, got it towed to an impound yard, and discovered that the thief had left his wallet on the front seat. Cops notified the owner who had to pay the tow and impound fees. Cops did nothing about following up with the thieves. Car theft is rampant here, with burned out cars proliferating. And garbage and used tires, in massive piles, are along the roadsides in the New Orleans vicinity. For the first time ever as far as I know, one of the people dumping tires on the roadside, about 14,000 in this case, got arrested. This was accomplished through the cooperative efforts of lots of agencies, including the Louisiana Department of Wildlife and Fisheries.

The letters to the editor drip with outrage. Never come back, they say. But it doesn't matter because there are enough new crops of visitors to mask the outrage. If all this ticketing were ratcheted down the city would not notice, but the human beings treated this way would feel so much better.

Starting with the small scale assault a newcomer faces, we have this. Getting a building permit was difficult and maddening. The city had plateaus where an application got parked for a month or so. Lawyers, contractors, and home-owners would be found sitting in the waiting room, for hours, for days, trying to pry the permit loose. The city required a small change in my plan that could have been penciled in and saved me a month of interest payments, if they had any concept of public service, which they never heard of apparently. But no, they put the whole plan in a pile for a letter to be written in a month telling me what I must do, and then another submission to the bottom of their pile. A phone call and a hand notation could have solved this to everyone's satisfaction in a few minutes. The city informed me that the front steps could not be more than 3 feet out. Mine were about 16 feet out. This caused quite the crisis and delay as our property was about 20 miles from central New Orleans, on a canal community, and plans had been drawn up by architect and engineer, for a traditional raised cottage, and what was wrong here. After long periods of anxiety and effort, it became clear that the person reviewing the plans had applied the requirements for the French Quarter to the house. If you have ever been to the French Quarter, this situation was so stupid as to be unbelievable.

The local newspaper, the Times Picayune, reports on the never-ending governmental stupidities the populace here must suffer. This particular point is cogent because our street, Murano Rd., has been flooded with salt water for about 20 years, at the end, affecting three occupied homes. Water is generally over a foot deep. The January 20, 2019 edition explained this. The drainage system is split between the sewer and water board {SWB) and the department of public works (DPW). SWB handles pipes larger than 36 inches, DPW smaller than 36 inches. This mess has stymied the correction of the flooding on my street because both agencies are involved and they just can't make it work, for this and related reasons.

We have boil water advisories routinely. Some of it is related to a rotten water infrastructure which will cost many millions to fix. Some is related to incompetence. The last two, just a few months ago, were investigated to see what happened. It was determined that two supervisors, on the two occasions, were found asleep on duty when pumps or some other remedy should have been instituted, but nothing was done. What was unusual in this water situation is that the two were fired or quit. But the process will not change; it is bedded in the concrete of tradition and as decades pass, and supervisors come and go, it appears that no capable person is examining the systems under which this city operates. One exception to this litany of doom is the Assessor's office, which has been reduced from five assessors to one, and that one, Errol Williams, has started a consistent method based on square footage. This information is posted on line for the public, reviewed, and leads to outrage wherever anyone finds that someone is not paying their fair share. As supervisors come and go, it appears that no capable person is examining the systems under which this city operates.

LiViN LAFFiN CRYiN DYiN
iN COASTAL
Louisiana
PART II

Most of this diary was lost during and after the Katrina catastrophe. We are blessed with it now due to the good offices of Guy and Elizabeth Thurmond, our lifelong friends, who preserved all of our correspondence, who, at the end of every message, said "Write a Book". OK, friends, here it is. Hammond

2003

June 27, 2003

This is such a strange place to live, I started writing it up. Thought I would share it with you occasionally. Please do NOT pass it on. Most of this is from the newspaper, and there is no limit to how lurid something is that is still printed. Some are my observations. The Governor, Mike Foster, got incensed with some legislators and other detractors from his plans, and called them a bunch of "hooligans, cuckoos, and whatnots". Gov. Foster is about74 years old, and as governor, apparently decided he needed something to occupy his mind and his time, so he has enrolled in law school. He rides a Harley without helmet on occasion, and was instrumental in changing the law to allow that for all. Quite the contribution to humanity.

I live way beyond what is normally viewed as New Orleans, even though technically it is within the city limits. Our place is on the water overlooking a marsh that is a wildlife refuge. But every day I drove down US Route 90 into and through eastern New Orleans to get to work. Along this route, there were three ho houses (houses of ill repute, or whore houses, or brothels) that were apparent to the innocent but observant citizen. Also, there was an X-rated peep show type, a block building with no windows, about 40 x 50 feet dimensions. The local community around there got active and rousted the ho houses out of business somehow. Tabu was a wood frame two story house without a porch, what might have been a family dwelling 50 years ago. The locals got it and turned it into a church, without a steeple. They painted the whole thing road-stripe yellow, except for the shutters which decorated

127

every window. They painted them bright purple. It makes the imagination run amuck to think of the confliction of spirits that reside in those buildings now.

As for the peep show building, the cops raided it while it was doing business, which seemed to be always. Inside that building, according to the newspaper, was a warren of little rooms where people could sit in privacy and participate in whatever the program may offer. During the raid, the cops caught a state legislator who was also a doctor in the adjoining parish (county) as well as the head of the local medical society. He had a wife and several children. All this was in the Times Picayune. This is an instance where we would hope that children were not keeping up with the Times.

A minister who was on Bourbon street several months ago observed gays engaged on the street, in full view of everyone in the vicinity. He filmed this, and sent the film hither and yon in an effort to get another law passed to prohibit this sort of thing. He succeeded in the getting a law. But the wording stipulates that the sexual act must be for the purpose of public exhibition. Otherwise it is ok. Can you imagine how this public exhibition part would be argued in court, as each side attempts to prove what the perps were thinking? If they were just enjoying themselves in public, that's ok, but if they were showing off, it's off to the slammer for them.

Just prior to the 9/11 terrorist attack, 21 FBI agents in New Orleans were engaged in surveilling the notorious Canal Street Brothel. They spent 6 months on this. Finally, they busted the operation and were called upon to explain why they were spending their time and Federal money in such a task that is normally a State prerogative. They explained that it had an "interstate" element, in that some of the "ladies" went from town to town, including Atlanta, and therefore it was a Federal matter. Interstate intercourse by professionals is more of a problem than state intercourse, we can all see that, and how much more serious it would be.

The client list has never been revealed, but is said to contain prominent citizens. The hos charged $300 per hour at that time. One doctor was a client. This was revealed when he was prosecuted for Medicare fraud. He spent something like $350,000 of the proceeds at the Canal Street Brothel. In the brothel, running it in various ways, the owners, in fact, were three generations of women. That would be the grandmother, the mother and the daughter. The grandmother did whatever and cooked for the weary clients so they could go back at it when restored. The mother did whatever, and handled the finances. The daughter was very active with whatever, which led the clients to go to the grandmother for some nourishment. (Update, October, 2004: There is now a movie being made, called, "The Canal Street Brothel" July, 2003.

Two young men decided to steal a car and looked around till they found one with the keys in it, a Honda. So, they took it and while riding around, decided to go see their girlfriend who worked in the sheriff's office in the court house. They went there, parked at the court house, went in and chatted with the girl, and returned to their stolen car where they discovered that they had locked the keys in the car. They then proceeded to try to break into the car, right outside the sheriff's office, and surprise, surprise, got nabbed in the act by the cops.

A teenage girl was shot by the cops while in her bedroom. This came about as follows. This house contained this girl and a couple, married or unmarried, parents of the girl, is not mentioned. One morning the girl left for school, or so everyone thought, and the couple, a bit later, left the house for an hour or so. This couple locked all doors from the inside except for the back door, which they locked from the outside with a padlock. Upon returning, the couple found that the padlock had been ripped off the door, so they called the cops. The cops entered, guns drawn, and called out for anyone inside to identify themselves and come out. There was no response. The house was largely dark inside, so the cops started going from room to room, searching. Seeing some movement in the dark in one of the rooms, and seeing something in the hand of that person in the dark who was moving, the cops fired a shot at the person, hitting the girl, who was standing in the dark, talking on a cell phone, not responding to the cops call for her to come out. So, she got shot in the leg. Turns out that she did not go to school, but returned home, unbeknownst to her parents or whatever they were, broke in to the house, apparently for not having a key to the house.

A uniformed highway patrol officer was in a convenience store fixing a hot-dog when a local fellow approached him and started talking about how stupid some criminals are, just asking to get caught. He wanted the officer to go along with this and give him a few examples, in the officer's experience, that fit this scenario. After they had talked along these lines for a while, the cop noticed a clear plastic bag containing a brown tobacco-like material hanging out of the pocket of this fellow. The cop started asking questions about what was in this bag, and eventually the fellow admitted that it was marijuana. So, the cop arrested him and observed that the idea of stupid behaviors certainly got some people caught.

August 07, 2003

Judge Hunter wanted to raise some money, so he had a bunch of tickets printed up with $250 printed on them. These are not tickets to anything, he just made them up and ordered every employee under him to sell them for the face amount and give him the money. Each person had about 10 they had to sell. He said he would fire them if they failed. He went to various events and pressured people to buy them from him, which is illegal. As to the employees, word of this eventually seeped out. He fired one person over it. That person explained the Judges scheme. The judge, a guy about 40, proclaimed to the media that the employee was just disgruntled and was disparaging a respected judge. Judge Hunter was questioned under oath about it and denied it all. However, the fired employee had made a tape recording of the Judge ordering her to do this. That was made available to the DA. This matter has moved through one level of the judicial system here with no action taken against the Judge. It was moved to a higher level. The matter will be taken under consideration at some vague point in the future. After that, the Judge was still practicing as Judge, warning people not to lie under oath.

Judge Bodenheimer was trafficking in drugs, having sex with a drug dealers' girlfriend while the dealer was on the premises, he says, as an explanation that he was not involved with the big bags of marijuana at the site. He was under house arrest when this was written and as of now it and all its multifaceted extensions have passed through the court system, not to the Judge's well being

Judge Green was videotaped and recorded receiving an envelope with $5000 cash in it, which, upon being asked by the bail bondsman offering the bribe, if it were OK to give him the money, said, "Rick, I think so", at which time he reached out and got the money. This is illegal, and if it were a campaign contribution then it exceeded the limit and would have been required to be given to a campaign committee and accounted for. After he got caught at this, months later, he declared that it was a campaign contribution but since it violated some other provision, he gave $5000 to the donor. He still continued running a courtroom. (Update, October 2004: Judge Green was under indictment on various bribery and racketeering schemes, but at that time was still running the state court. The newspaper has opined that there is something wrong with this picture.)

A woman judge got involved in some kickback scheme that was publicized in the Times Picayune (TP). At that point, there was no apparent effect on her judgeship.

There is a 25-mile-long bridge that goes north from New Orleans across Lake Pontchartrain to a little town at the other end. It is a toll bridge; which thousands of cars cross each way each day. Everyone has to pay a toll except for those that have some sort of connection, which is lots of people. One provision was that law enforcement officers could show a badge and cross the bridge free. The chief of police of the little town at the other end of the bridge had been selling city police badges to various people for $1000 each. These fake cops would flash their badges at the toll booths to avoid paying the tolls.

Eventually, the toll booth people began to get suspicious about how many cops that little town had. Now the media have exposed it.

A while back, with regard to charges by a woman that she was raped by the New Orleans police, she testified that this cop raped her both on the first and the second dates.

The Public Service Commission (PSC) sets rates for various things that serve the public, including utilities etc. The businesses that the PSC regulates had been providing all sorts of perks to members of the PSC, including meals, travel, spas, hotels, sports events, etc. The PSC was headed by "Tubby" LeBlanc. An electric utility, just one of the many outfits providing these perks, has provided Tubby with 154 meals at a cost of about $3500, over the past year. That is about $23 per meal for Tubby, every other day throughout the year, just from the one utility. Tubby says there is nothing wrong with this, and he is providing a good service to the citizens. Various law enforcement entities have said there is nothing illegal about it. The legislature has said there are no ethics provisions that have been put in place to apply here.

2004

June 21, 2004

Went shrimping couple of days ago and got 210 pounds. Went fishing and caught some nice trout one day, nice redfish the next day, and for the first time did not grill the redfish so long as to turn them into a rubber tire, so they did taste good.

Was sitting on the patio idly looking across the water when in drifted an orange thing with a green top, looked like a little raft with a green hat on it. So, I watched it off and on for a few hours and wondered why it did not drift on somewhere else, like was it anchored somehow. Finally decided to investigate, whipped off my sandals and jumped off the dock feet down, and landed right on some very large oysters sticking straight up, wondered why I did not cut off my leg with this, but the oysters were a bit dull and nothing got cut. I got to wondering what they could be growing on, considering the silty nature of the bottom, so dove down and pulled out the thing buried in the mud that they were attached to. It turned out to be the stock of a rifle or shotgun. Dove some more, looking for the barrel or other parts, but just came up with an assortment of stuff like oyster shells, pine cones, palm leaves, sticks. Put the gunstock on the dock and got back to the other investigative task of swimming out to see what the orange and green thing were. That turned out to be a brand-new life vest (orange) still wrapped in the plastic packaging from the store, labels and tags hanging from it, with a green plastic container of Quaker State oil perched atop it. Just how that bottle stayed upright, where this came from, why it stopped its journey where it did and stayed there for quite a

133

while was unfathomable, but it did not stop me from trying to fathom it. Gunstock still on the dock awaiting further examination, which was deferred when the shrimp boat turned over in the canal about 4 am. It was trying to poach some shrimp from the refuge, which my house overlooks, using some wide rigging with nets and frames that stick out from both sides up near the bow, and skim the surface. Apparently one of these wing nets hung up on something on the bottom, and before the thieves could throttle back, the boat tilted left and swamped, got lodged on the bottom, parts sticking above water, blocking part of a commercial waterway. About 12 hours later the coast guard showed up, two boats, 6 people, sat there afloat pondering the situation for a couple of hours, then a coast guard helicopter showed up and hovered and searched for an hour or so, maybe looking for bodies.

Then we learned from the Coast Guard that the owner of the shrimp boat had been contacted. He claimed the boat had been stolen. So, someone steals a strange (I would presume) shrimp boat, gets it started and operational with crew, departs with it from its berth, goes over to the wildlife refuge canal and starts shrimping at 4am? I guess that's plausible, considering that this is Louisiana.

While tramping across the neighbor's property to observe all this, one of the neighbors gave me a rather hefty insulated water cooler jug full of margarita to sip on. After I drank about a quart of this stuff, I was too uncoordinated and out of focus to continue the cast net I was rebuilding on my patio. I had stopped the epoxy work on the sailboat to go fishing, so that was waiting to be finished also, but there was yet more fishing to be done, there is the cast net to finish, the gunstock to investigate, the life preserver to do something with, and the need for a continuing inspection of the shrimp boat situation to see where the tides carry it since no one secured it, and I surely want to be present where they try to raise it or whatever it turns out that they do with it. The coast guard put a buoy out from it, rather far out in my view, thus posing more of an impediment than the shrimp boat, but highway cops do that too with their cars and they probably go to school at the same place to learn this technique. So, as you can see, the work just piles up and I am getting more and more in arrears on this stuff. I have no doubt that if I am alert, something of interest will present itself today to compound my problems.

November 22, 2004

Three young men were looking for their rivals, roaming about New Orleans with AK47 semi auto assault weapons. They thought the enemy was in a white Mercedes, and came upon such a vehicle about to enter a car wash in the territory they all hung out in. So, they opened up and riddled the car with bullets, shooting from several vantage points and moving about and shooting some more. Unbeknownst to them, however, the car wash had video cameras in several locations, and all this activity was captured on film. The reproduction quality was such that the shooters could be easily identified, the police did identify them, and picked them up and put them in jail. The tapes were run on television here, and you could see the shooters standing there blazing away at the car. Incidentally, they were wrong about who was in the car, it was just some innocent people who had nothing to do with these events. This case eventually came to the court of Judge Arthur Hunter, who declared that he would not admit the videotape as evidence, so he turned all three shooters loose. Within two weeks, one of the three shot and killed another person, so was arrested again

Public outcry was incessant and the citizens were outraged. It turns out that of about twelve judges that handle such cases, where the case is tried by the judge and not a jury, that three of the judges dismiss 66 percent of the cases brought before them. The other nine judges dismiss only about 16 percent. The national average for this sort of thing is about 9 percent.

Another judge Hunter, reported on earlier, made his employees sell tickets he had printed up for $250 each and give him the money. The tickets were no to anything, had no value. He later, after lots of lying under oath and accusing others, said he should not be removed as judge because the only other thing he could do was roofing, which he did before becoming a crooked judge, and he was now to old and fat to go back to that so he should be allowed to continue as judge.

Judge Ronnie Bodenheimer, owner of our neighborhood marina, was jailed.

Judge Alan Green was videotaped by the FBI on two occasions taking $5000 bribes from a bail bondsman in exchange for steering prospective clients to the bondsman, and other considerations. Further investigation by the FBI produced a list of 20 or 30 other forms of payoffs to Judge Green by the same outfit, vacations, golf outings, car repairs etc. Lawyer for Judge Green says it's all bullshit.

A state district judge was invited to a costume party in a public restaurant, open to the public at the time of the party. The judge decided to go as a black man, so he blackened his face. Furthermore, he decided to go as a black prison inmate, so in addition to the black face and hands, he got a set of jail coveralls with something like "prison inmate" written on them, got some shackles which he wore, and an afro wig, and went to the party. The black community was outraged, suggesting that the judge has a preconceived notion about blacks and maybe he could not give them a fair trial. This judge had been on the bench for 20 years. Just where this is going is unknown at this point.

A security guard at a video poker parlor decided to steal the money from the machines while she was on duty and had the opportunity. So, she blacked out the security cameras, broke into the machines, got about $70,000 cash, sacked it up, and threw it in or near a creek where she intended to recover it later. She reported to the police that a gang had come in and robbed the place. The police got wind somehow that some stolen money was in or around the creek, so they went looking for it. They found a beaver pond at the site, and decided to tear into the beaver dam so they could lower the water level and look for the money. In tearing up the dam, they found it was made partly of cash paper money, intact, and stuffed here and there as part of the dam. Turns out that the beavers found the sacks of money, opened them, got the money out and used it in their dam, without damaging the money. The police arrested 3 adult beavers, which was two males and one female, and 4 pups, for packing a dam with the illegal proceeds from a gambling operation. OK that last line is a joke, but at this point I bet you were ready to go for it.

Former Governor Edwin Edwards was imprisoned for extorting money for riverboat gambling licenses. He corrupted his son, who was also jailed. But, some time back, the FBI had videotaped the governor giving a person named Cleo Fields about $24,000 cash payoff. In a minor little side play, the FBI camera operator forgot to turn on the camera to catch the Gov actually handing over the money, but shortly thereafter realized this little glitch and turned it on. The bulk of the cash was so voluminous, however, that Cleo had a real hard time stuffing it all into his pockets, and finally, with the camera rolling, that part was captured. Cleo has never denied this, simply saying that he was a private person and it was no one's business. He has not been charged.

Cleo served in the US Congress in the 1990's and ran for governor in 1995. He was not elected, but after being videotaped taking the money, was elected twice to the state senate, despite widespread publication of this payoff. A few months later he decided that he wanted to be on the Public Service Commission, and ran for election against a fellow named Bossiere. Cleo apparently wanted some of the graft from the PSC, in the form of thousands of dollars in meals provided and other considerations, as with another PSC commissioner named Tubby Le Blanc. Bossiere got the videotape of Fields taking the money from Gov Edwards and ran it in his campaign. Eventually, after a runoff, we got Cleo out of the picture and now we have Bossiere. It was later revealed that Bossiere, who was constable of 1st City Court of New Orleans, improperly took $41,000 in illegal salary advances. He claimed he did nothing wrong, that lots of others had done it too. Turns out that this is a common practice, and that it is illegal. James Lee Burke, a bestselling novelist, has cranked out another Dave Robicheaux novel about New Orleans. In it, he declares that New Orleans is an outdoor insane asylum built on a giant sponge.

December 9, 2004

Nick Stipelcovich is the world record holder for crawfish eating and a multiple champion of the Breaux Bridge Crawfish Eating Festival. He had many accomplishments, was featured in various magazines including National Geographic, for fund-raising for charities, and for eating. He was a member of the international Federation of competitive eaters, held a worldwide rank of 49th in this competition, and was known as Crawfish Nick. His record eating involved scoffing up 55 3/4 pounds of crawfish in 45 minutes. He says it's all a matter of speed, combined with technique and concentration, gettem in just as fast as you can. Nick died a few days ago at the age of 54.

Some of the details of this next event escape me, since I was negligent and did not record it at the time. But, a couple of weeks ago a city attorney was fired for raping a woman in his office. The rapee-to-be was caught messing around with her boyfriend in city park, with some off her clothing a bit off, and was cited for lewd conduct or some such. The legal proceedings eventually brought her into contact with the city attorney in his office in the courthouse, where the attorney explained that things might go badly unless she went over to his other office where he had his private practice. A few days later she met him there as he instructed her to, whereupon he flung her face-down on the sofa and raped her. When this was over, she left, and unbeknownst to the lawyer, reported it to the police. Days later, the attorney, egotist that he apparently was, thinking the rapee enjoyed the experience, or was what, stupid? called her again and told her to go to his office again or she would be in big trouble. The cops kept the date with the attorney, who was strongly politically connected to the past mayoral administration of Marc Morial. So, the attorney got arrested. Turns out that 6 years prior he had been accused of raping another woman in his office, but the attorney general at the time declined to prosecute.

And speaking of the attorney general's office, an assistant DA just got fired for extortion. Turns out that she was friends or something with a painter who would make a deal with some homeowner to do a job for a certain amount, in this instance $1000. Later, the painter would return and demand more money, $300 in this instance, for what he described as cost overruns. Homeowner declined to pay, so this assistant DA started calling and threatening prosecution, calling as much as 8 times a day. Meanwhile, the homeowner had a live-in girlfriend who became frightened by all these threats, and while her boyfriend was out, upon the occasion of the painter demanding more money, she wrote out a check on their joint account for the money demanded. The homeowner/boyfriend had not instructed her about this mess, nor the fact that he had closed out the checking account. So, the painter now had a bad check, which he said caused him to incur even more costs, so the assistant DA then upped the extortion demands on threat of jail time. Well, we will see who goes to jail. I don't know the outcome. The crusading newspaper, the Time Picayune, says all this is really bad stuff, that we can't have the local government lawyers raping and extorting people

About 2 months ago, my neighbor Moon Mullens and I were coming back from a fishing trip, wherein I caught 13 nice ones and he didn't catch a dam thing, when we spotted a bait well adrift in the middle of Chef Menteur River, also known as Chef Pass. This thing is about 3 feet on a side, a cube of vinyl covered steel mesh within a PVC framework, meant to be tied to your dock as a place to store live bait; maybe ripped loose by the last hurricane. Since I needed one, we went after it. Moon heaved it up on the bow, where it was of sufficient size that I could not see directly where we were going, however, it is a big river, so that was OK. Moon said all this was embarrassing. People would see that thing on the bow and think this was how we ordinarily went fishing, by taking the whole bait well with us perched on the bow. While he was getting all red-faced over this, and while I was thinking that maybe it is possible to embarrass a cajun about some particular thing, I saw something jumping around in the cage. So, we stopped and opened er up and found about a dozen live shrimp jumping around in it. We tried fishing with them for a while to no avail, then went home where I dropped the cage off my dock and tied it on. Didn't look back in it till yesterday, just as it was getting dark, and was astonished to find 3 live shrimp still in it. So, I stopped what I was doing, which was fixing supper of steamed crabs and fried oysters, and started fishing with one of the shrimp. Moon came out and told me it was too late in the day to be fishing for our supper and got a good laugh out of it. He walked off with a condescending chuckle to take a shower. About 2 minutes later my float started skimming across the water and by and by I landed a nice large freshwater largemouth bass, in salt water, with a live shrimp. Moon descended from his stilt house and came to stare it is, admitting that he was wrong once again. So, for supper, we had the steamed crabs, the fried oysters and the fried freshwater bass fillets.

2005

February 7, 2005

Today's summary has a little update about the local stuff, and a bit about the National in relation to coal mining and corruption therein.

As for New Orleans--

A couple of cops decided to extort money from various unfortunates who crossed their paths in the course of their policing. Their grand plan was to catch a fellow, and it's not clear whether they actually had to be breaking the law, or whether there were some other criteria. Anyway, they threatened the victim till they made him/her go to and ATM machine and withdraw $300 cash and hand it over. To ensure that the victim did not just run off, one of the cops accompanied the victim to the ATM machine. This went on for a while, but finally one of the victims went to some other cops, who investigated. The investigators located one or more ATMs that had been used in the extortion and got the video recording of the transaction, wherein the crooked cop was seen to be standing right beside the victim making him take out the money. By and by this led to the arrest of both cops and the discovery of even more extortions they had committed.

A couple of fellows were holed up in an amorous situation at a motel here. About 3am, history shows, some major hostilities developed in the little room, and both men ran out of the room naked, into the parking lot, where one chased the other round and round till he caught the other, and killed him. The person killed, naked in the parking lot, was a New Orleans cop, it was eventually discovered.

A New Orleans cop stopped a nice-looking young lady, and in the course of citing some minor traffic violation, explained to her that this was bad business she was caught up in, that the consequences could be dire, but if she would be cooperative, he could protect her from those out to get her, and this protection would have to be long term proposition, and she had to tell him where she lived, what her home phone number was, and agree to cooperate with him. So, he turned her loose under these conditions, and over the course of some days or weeks, kept calling her at home, and demanding that she come down to the street and get in the car with him.

The young lady, and her mother, contacted the police about all this, and the other cops started coaching her, and tapped the phone lines. They gathered that evidence, and asked her to go meet the bad cop as this situation matured. So, she agreed, next time the bad cop called, to meet him on the street. He showed up in uniform, in a marked police car, told her to get in, and then drove her into the depths of a deserted industrial area of warehouses and defunct businesses, and proceeded to try to force himself on her. She resisted, and eventually the bad cop took her back to her apartment. He was arrested later that night.

And for a bit of national news
February 07, 2005 9:22 AM
Subject: checkup
I appreciate how you have been keeping me entertained, so here is my effort to reciprocate. In the narrative below, Griles is the Deputy Secretary of the Interior, still getting paid by the coal companies he is supposed to regulate, and all this has been deemed as no conflict of interest by the Secretary, Gale Norton, and the current administration. Jack is Jack Spadaro, one of your neighbors, working out of Hamlin now. Was previously Administrator of the Mine Health and Safety Academy in Beckley, but was fired for revealing corruption in the investigation of a mine waste slurry impoundment that failed a few years ago and wiped out homes and a watershed in SW W. VA., and for blowing the whistle on a deal Admin friends of Bush used to circumvent

competitive bidding by demanding the issuance of something like 180 $2499 no-bid contracts to one of their friends. All this was on 60 minutes last fall where Jack was interviewed. You may have seen his name in the Gazette. Expect to see more of it

February 07, 2005 9:12 AM

Jack--

Send me your celestial transporter coordinates and I will transport myself over there and we will have a heck of a time. Back in Charleston, when The Office of Surface Mining Reclamation and Enforcement, US Department of the Interior, was setting up that office, I heard a few things about you--didn't trust the damn bureaucrats, tried to tell the truth if truth could be determined, and went your own way regardless of the politics. So, I made arrangements for you to be put in my work area. And see what happened.----

In terms of someone going stark raving mad, they can't get to you now short of hiring an assassin, so you are free to drive them stark raving mad and they can't fire you. Here is some biology for you to keep in the back of your mind when any of your activities might reach as high as Griles, and people will wonder why you are smiling. Another thing, since your enemies are my enemies too, I can smile too.

When you bring on some anxiety for Griles and his kin, here is what happens in their damn body. The adrenalin gets pumping. The short-term effects are constriction of the peripheral blood vessels, increased heart rate, rerouting the blood flow away from digestion (gut) and toward musculature. So, the food sits in their stomach like a cantaloupe. Or watermelon, depending on how puffed up they are. Also, the anger needs some outlet, so its leave the office with some friends and go eat, and get each other pumped up over just what Spadero is telling people. This causes them to overeat and overdrink, but since the adrenalin is pumping and digestion has shut down, they just get constipated, which interferes with their sleep and makes them walk funny. The eating, since I am sure it's not salads, leads to high fat and cholesterol intake

143

which leads to arthrosclerosis which leads to high blood pressure which leads to strokes, heart attacks and impotence. One thing feeds the other.

The long-term effects of increased adrenalin output are enlarged adrenal glands, and the adrenalin itself, in the long term, with overproduction, damages most organs in the abdomen, leading them even further down the long-term path toward misery. So, keep up the good work.

Regards, Hammond.

March 01, 2005

From: "Chew, Dennis"

Hammond:

Good to hear from you. I see from your writing style you have not changed much. Having worked in MS for 10 years, I am very familiar with the Chandeleurs, as well as Horn and Ship Islands. Those sand bars can be problematic. I was involved in some research on Horn Island. We used to go out in a 30-40 ft boat, anchor off the island, and wade in. One time, there were literally dozens of big bull sharks cruising between the bars; it is easier for them to herd mullet and other prey between these bars. We just had to wait until they left, but I was a nervous wreck when we finally waded in. I've also flown over these areas and seen many sharks and thousands of stingrays during certain times of the year.

Dennis

March 23, 2005 Wildlife Hike

Mention some alligators to one person and he then demands details. May as well do the whole thing.

My 4-mile hike yesterday was along a levee surrounded by swamps and lakes and old waterways along the levees. Saw 6 gators and a cottonmouth moccasin, among other things. One of them was rather large, about 10 feet, with the fixed grin at the back of its jaws, watching me with its head raised up. That would be one of the gators. The moccasin was right in my path, determined not to move. As I approached, he raised his head, apparently thinking he was a cobra, and signaling he had no intention of turning tail. Kind of flared out his jaws making his head look quite triangular. It was clearly a mano a mano proposition, but I decided to be charitable and relieve him of the worry of where his next meal would come from. Since the area is well patrolled by hawks, vultures, crows, and the occasional eagle, not to mention hogs, I relieved something else of the worry of where its next meal would come from also. It was a beautiful morning.

The gators are generally immobile, some crawled up on something so the whole body is visible, some mostly submerged along an edge, lurking, a few slowly swimming along. There are large masses of aquatic vegetation with round leaves like a small lily pad, matted together in big rafts with open water areas in their midst. Lots of purple gallinules, with their purple body, coral beak with white tip, spreading their toes on these pads and walking along feeding. The gators are scattered all over the same area. Gators can strike, moving forward, and to do so, their whole body has to move. Some of these gators are probably 400 pounds. That's a lot of inertia to overcome. They also strike sideways, and in this instance, the bulk of their body does not get displaced. Thinking of it from an engineering perspective, if they lunge their head to the right to snap up a gallinule, and switch the tail to the right also, the tail would prevent a counter rotation effect and enhance the strike. That's my theory, anyway. I did not see any of them get a gallinule, and wonder if they ever do.

There were lots of ducks, the most beautiful being the wood duck, but it is a close contest. The most ridiculous is the coot. That is a black sort of ducklike bird with a white chicken beak, about the size of a bantam hen. They feed along the edges of clusters of reeds, and wait till you are right next to them before they decide to attempt to fly. What you hear then is a repetitive pounding sound of feathers beating on the water, and what you see, as this thing

145

moves out from behind the reeds, is a mighty struggle to get airborne. They are pounding the water with their wings as they move forward, each impact leaving twin round ripples like a stone thrown in the water, and these pairs of ripples are then strung out along its attempted flight path in growing circles. Underneath this bird, you have his legs stretched out as far as he can reach downward, trying to run across the top of the water. So, its legs windmilling frantically, wings beating furiously, for about 50 feet before it finally gets a few inches up and clears the water. I can't help laughing at the damn things.

There are lots of white ibises, in flocks, long decurved pink bill, probing the mud, sometimes putting their whole head under. Some (black colored) glossy ibises, tricolor herons, great white and snowy egrets, great blue herons and little blue herons, and lots of hawks, mostly buteos. There are plenty of hair-laden scats, or droppings, all along the trail. Looks like rabbit hair, or maybe rat hair, from a distance, heh heh. Saw some fox tracks, dog tracks, hog tracks. Well, that's what my neighborhood is like. Is yours any different?

May 4, 2005 Green et al

You may recall Judge Alan Green, who was videotaped by FBI surveillance, pocketing envelopes stuffed with $5000 cash, on two occasions. These were bribes by a bail bondsman who wanted business directed his way. Later there were other bribes identified, maybe 20 or so, specifically, detailing exactly what was involved, dates and amounts. These bribes totaled $20,000 cash, meals and golf rounds. Well, justice grinds forward and now. Judge Green has a "legal team" to deal with his trial, which is in a few months. Among those on his legal team is a former prosecutor turned defense attorney, now located way up north, maybe Minnesota. This guy conducted an interview with the media here, from his location up there, and said this whole thing about Judge Green was race-based. (Judge Green is black) The Minnesota lawyer said everyone knows how corrupt Louisiana is, and the charging of Judge Green is just one more example of it, and he (the lawyer) is going to come down here and investigate this matter of going after Judge Green just cause he is black. He calls it selective prosecution.

The way Judge Green corrupted the system is revealed in wiretaps made public. Green, and I am going to quit calling him Judge even though he continued to be paid over 100K annually years after all this came to light, was out playing golf. Meantime, back at the jail, Corey Miller, known as rapper C-Murder, brother of rap star Master P, was being held for second degree murder. The crooked bail bondsman, Bowley, employee of crooked bail bondsman Marcotte, phoned Green out on the golf course to discuss what bail to set. Since Corey Miller was thought to be able to get a pile of money to pay a bail, the discussion was just how high a bail the crooked bail bondsman could cover. Green asked them what the figure they could cover would be, and the crooked bail bondsman said, "we could make a million-dollar bond if you could set it". Green said "All right....Okey doke", then set the bond at $1,005,000. I find the precision of this figure striking. What's with the $5,000 addon, I wonder? An attempt to give the impression of something carefully calculated?

The defense team for Green has come up with a real mind-boggler, and they present it with a straight face. They said that the wiretaps used to trap Green in this bail bond complicity were not justified by previous wiretaps which did not suggest that further wiretaps would reveal that Green was likely to discuss some illegal activity in these further wiretaps. The wiretaps used to justify further wiretaps, those said to be inadequate in their suggestiveness of further criminal activity on Green's part, involve a conversation between Green and U. S. Representative William Jefferson, D-New Orleans, wherein Jefferson is asking Green to do some fundraising for his (Jefferson's) daughter's successful campaign for the state Legislature. Green said he had to be careful about that stuff, and Jefferson said "Well, you know who you can call and who you can't". Louisiana code says a judge may not solicit funds for, pay for, make contributions to a political organization or candidate or purchase tickets, etc. As to the FBI videotape wherein Bowley was imaged handing over an envelope with $5,000 cash, twice, the defense is that the FBI should not have been granted the access needed to make the tape. Green was shown to have deposited a bit over half of this cash in his personal checking account within about a week of getting it. Months after getting it, or maybe many months when all this started coming out, Green said it was a campaign contribution and he then returned $5,000 to the crooked bail bondsman.

It was gratifying to discover that Green was living well beyond his means, even with this illegal income supplement, and it was only a matter of time before his house came tumbling down. Wonder what he could possibly have been thinking about all this?

By the way, the former governor, Edwin Edwards was imprisoned, put there by the same FBI team going after Green. The 3 former insurance commissioners also went to prison.

Speaking of insurance commissioners, the law here is such that the commissioner can get any kind of wheels he wants without anyone's approval, and charge it to the taxpayer. Robert Wooley was one. He ordered himself a Ford SUV, Eddie Bauer interior, all sorts of accessories, for $40,000. Got tired of it apparently, and next ordered a Ford pickup, King Cab, heated leather seats, 6 position CD player, a rack of lights on the roof, a tow and camper package, and flames painted all down the side. This one was discounted for the taxpayer, and he got it for $40,000 also. There has been quite the furor over this, and Mr. Wooley, ever the sensitive public servant, proclaimed that this is all "just a pimple on a bees ass". And besides, he put 30,000 miles on the SUV, and it was time for another truck. Lots of bills have been introduced into the legislature to get Mr. Wooley out of the truck buying business.

In Florida, this beautiful, blonde young woman decided she wanted to go to New Orleans to get a job and have some fun. Her daddy told her it was a bad idea, that New Orleans was a dangerous place and she could get hurt. Paying no heed to her daddy, she came here, got a job as a waitress. Couple weeks ago, she and a friend took a cab from the restaurant where they worked, to their residence. They got out of the cab about 4 blocks from where she was staying, around 1am. Why they did not get cabbed right to their door is a mystery. As they were walking along the street, they were approached by a couple of young males who asked directions to somewhere. The two young women tried to help them, but before long it turned into a robbery where the thief was fighting to get their purses, both of which were held by the young women. The Florida woman got shot in the head and died next day in a local hospital. The men ran off with the purses, which contained, among other things, the aprons from the restaurant where the women worked. Now, what we have here is a crime committed at 1am on a dark street with no witnesses except the victims, one of which died, the other of which said they were black males about so high etc., which narrows it down to about a few hundred thousand or a million. What chance do the cops have of catching these guys? Zilch, you would think.

A few days or a week later, some young black guys showed up at an auto repair shop the get their jeep SUV type thing repaired. One thing led to another, and by and by it was discovered that this jeep was stolen. Also, there were two purses on the front seat, and they contained aprons from the restaurant where the two women victims of the robbery and murder previously mentioned, worked. Now the cops have the assailants identified, turns out that there are three. Apparently, they are all in custody (this point was not absolutely clear), one of the three having been arrested in the meantime for some other crime.

A New Orleans police officer, brandishing his gun and badge, broke into a house recently, entering the living room from the front door. He showed his badge, and pointed his gun at the people in the living room. The people there were two men and several women, in the living room. As best I can figure this out, he then sexually assaulted one of the women. pointing the gun, and showing the badge to the crowd. With the first woman done, he demanded the other woman for similar purposes, but this was a bit unclear. Anyway, she refused, and succumbed. Succumbed? What that mean, I wonder? Faint? She apparently did not die or one would have thought that would have been

149

mentioned. Unbeknownst to this amazing cop, there was yet another woman in another part of the house. When all this started, this other woman called 911. Another gang of cops arrived at the place while the first cop was still in the living room trying to continue his rampage.

The crusading newspaper noted that in the last few months, about half a dozen cops have been caught in various illegal enterprises, and how many others might there be, and maybe there is something wrong with the screening process for cops in New Orleans.

Eddie Jordan was on the FBI team that put the former Governor, Edwin Edwards, in prison. Jordan ran for and got elected District Attorney for New Orleans. One of his first official acts was to fire 56 people peremptorily, 53 of whom were white. He then hired 68 people, comprised of 92 percent black and 7 percent white. He got sued for racial discrimination.

In the various public statements he made, some on the same day, he said that he was trying to make the racial balance within his office mirror the racial composition of the city, then went on to say that in the firing and hiring he was not aware of what the race of anyone was and therefore he was innocent of bias. He went on to say that actual competence of those fired, and of those hired, did not figure into the firing and hiring, it was just a matter of getting people who were loyal to him hired. I guess the weight of the prosecution of Gov. Edwards must have been carried by other members of the team back when Jordan was doing that sort of thing.

Anyway, Jordan lost, obligated this near bankrupt city with millions in award and legal fees, and is now threatening-- threatening to appeal, to drag this out for years, that he has no money to pay the awards. Incidentally, he has 90 some odd assistant district attorneys, and he pays them about $31,000 per annum. Average length of service is 18 months. According to some city rule, he can't pay them more.

Bob Odum was the Agriculture Commissioner. Several decades ago it was worried about that big oil would sell gas at losing prices to drive out the little guys, then with the resulting sort of monopoly would raise gas prices outrageously. Never happened, the law was never enforced, no agency ever given authority to enforce it, and was forgotten, till just recently. When gas prices here went up to $2.10, Odum decided that, since he was responsible for weights and measures, which involved gas pumps, that while he was there at the gas station, he would start enforcing the law that said that no one could sell gas at less than a 6% markup. He became a fighter for higher gas prices, much to the dismay of dam near every man, woman, and child in Louisiana.

The crusading Times Picayune was outraged, as were all the columnists and the letters to the editor writers. The Governor, Ms. Blanco, was also outraged. Lots of bills were introduced to strip Odum of this power he was never given. All failed. He decided to build a sugar mill, and required all his employees to do the construction. We are talking about your average office worker, not a construction person, being bused daily to the construction site. Most everyone was outraged about this. Outraged about building the mill, outraged about how it was done, outraged at the accidents that were occurring. It continued. He was charged with about a dozen crimes. One by one, they all came to no avail. This is all so peculiar that writers were left gasping.

Well, now we come back to the notorious carwash shootings, where three black youths were caught very clearly on video tape, ambushing with AK-47's a couple of people in a Mercedes at the carwash. Mistaken identity, but never mind that. They riddled the car, somehow managed not to kill anyone. All this was played over TV here, over and over. When the case came up for charging the assailants, the Judge, Arthur Hunter, said the tape was inadmissible as evidence. Public outrage again. Hunter reconsidered, then set the bail at $50K, despite the appeals of Asst. DA Williams, who argued for $450K. Ms. Williams said it's the damndest thing she ever saw, and she has seen plenty, or words to that effect. Aside from Hunter's love for criminals and his desire to get killers back on the street, other things were going on in other jurisdictions. Of the three, one was charged by the Feds with a gun violation, so that stuck him in jail. Another was jailed for another murder after Judge Hunter turned him loose about the carwash shootings, so that put him in jail. The third one Washington, was allowed to remain free.

May 23, 2005 Shrimpin Cajun Style

Shrimp season started today, and we were in the shrimp boat and out of the canal before daylight, intending to pass the two swing bridges on our way to open waters of the bay. Went under the car bridge, were in the center of the river headed for the train bridge when the engine shut off. Tide was going out, carrying us toward the train bridge. I studied the drift situation to see just what the projection was, and discovered that we were going to be swept into the end of the cribwork that was intended to deflect all vessels from hitting the bridge pivot system, deflect them into the passage between the pivot system and the other side of the passage where a big foundation pillar was protected by another cribwork. The arresting thing about our projected drift was that the cribwork was wrecked by a previous collision with something mammoth, and instead of coming to a point, which a boat would drift up against and go harmlessly, more or less, around one side or the other and through the passage, there was a gap. The whole end of the cribwork was broken off, leaving a gap about 20 feet wide, an open jaw, so to speak, and about a 12-inch steel pipe about 4 feet above the water spanned the opening about 5 feet inside the opening. We were heading into this gap, and the cabin of the shrimp boat is what would come into the contact with the pipe, and once we got inside this cribwork we would be stuck there till the tide changed, assuming that the boat stayed afloat that long.

The shrimp boat skipper, my neighbor Moon, just stood there staring at the engine cover, occasionally trying to restart the engine, and saying "I don't know what to do with this engine". The whole thing about where we were drifting and what to do about that went unrecognized, as he never looked up to see what was happening. This boat is 26 feet long, 10 feet wide, and weighs

7000 pounds. We were about a hundred yards from the cribwork. He had one old oar on the boat. I got that out and started paddling furiously with it, trying to move the boat the 30 feet required to get past the cribwork. It slowly moved forward and we cleared the obstacle, drifting through the intended bridge passage. That left us drifting in mid river, so I just kept paddling, aiming for shallow water about another 50-75 yards away. Asked Moon to get out the anchor, and discovered that he had no more than about 20 feet of line on the anchor. The river was about 50 feet deep at this point, 80 feet deep further on. I finally had to paddle within just a few feet of the marsh before the anchor caught.

All the other shrimpers were streaming past, and who would want to stop at a time like that to help someone. Well, no one would, including ourselves, had we been mobile.

Moon decided the engine was not getting gas, so he took the cover off, and the air filter, to get at the carburetor, then from a spare container poured out about a half pint of gas into a little can. Cranking away with the starter, he poured this gas into the carb at a trickle. Engine would not start. He decided the points were off, or burned, so we took off the distributor cap to check. It was dark still, and we had no flashlight, so this was largely futile. He thought the gap should be about .040 inches and asked me to try to set the points at that. I did so, we cranked her over, but no spark at the points. We later found that the setting was supposed to be .016. I put the cap back on, took a spark plug wire off, stuck a screw driver down into the end of the wire to make electrical contact, and held the shaft of the screwdriver against an engine bolt ground to check for spark, and got none. I started by trial and error closing the point gap down till a spark occurred, and finally got a weak yellow spark at the plug, all this being done in the dark. Still would not start, so Moon poured more gas in the carburetor. I thought it would be flooded by this time, and stuck my fingers into the carb to open the flaps while he was to crank it over. He suggested that I use a couple of long screwdrivers for this instead of my fingers, so I did it that way. He cranked her over, a blast of fire came out of the carb, and shortly thereafter it was running. We did not at this point, nor throughout the day, ever figure out what the main culprit was.

This was a 455-cu inch engine from a junked 1970 '98 Oldsmobile that was abandoned in someone's yard out in the country for a couple of decades. Moon bought the car for $300 and had a wrecker deliver it to his home. Probably took him, with occasional help from me, nearly a year to get it out of the car, rebuilt, and into his shrimp boat to replace a similar one that conked out earlier. All these options to get it running, i.e., fuel supply, spark, points, carb, flaps, flooding, clearing the flooding, pouring gas in the carb, were what people went through before electronics came along and rendered us all helpless in this regard.

The question at this point, engine running but we did not know why, was, do we go shrimping, or go home. We opted for shrimping, or, more accurately, Moon did. I got to wondering if something on the carb might be sticking and asked Moon if he had any WD40. WD40 comes in a blue spray can. Moon pointed to the shelf across the front of the cockpit, and said yeah, right there. I looked around and all to be seen was a green spray can of OFF insect repellent. I told him that was OFF, not WD40, and he said well, it's up there somewhere.

We got out there in Borgne Bay, dragged for an hour, pulled up the net, and the engine shut off. Went through the entire drill again, all the individual elements of it, with one addition. He decided the fuel filter must be stopped up, but he had a spare, he said. We took the old one off and discovered that the tubes sticking out from the new one were too small to fit tightly over the larger rubber hoses they were inserted into, so after the replacement, we had a steady stream of gasoline leaking into the bilge under the engine. I fooled around with that and some hose clamps and eventually stopped more leakage from occurring. I suggested that Moon get the WD40 and spray down the carb and see if we could get the choke flaps going again. He got the green can of OFF and sprayed the hell out of that carb. I watched him for a while in amazement. Finally told him he was using OFF, that WD40 came in a blue can. He kind of acted like it was all one and the same. Engine still would not start after spraying it with OFF. In the end, it was stick the screwdrivers into the carb and crank her over. Got it going that way, and did another drag. Engine shut off again when we pulled in the net. By this time, we were probably 8 miles from home. It was clearly time to quit this operation before we got stranded, but Moon wanted to pull on the way home. We did so, crossed the Bay this way, but engine shut off again when we pulled in the net.

Went through it all again, got it started, got into the river system, and it started putting out a black cloud of smoke--other shrimpers were staring. Moon went slowly along the side of the rivers, through the bridges, into our canal system, and as he got it aimed at his dock, it shut off again, and this was final. We had enough momentum to carry us to the dock, where we discovered that the incessant grinding with the starter had stripped the gears off the shaft and it was to be started no more.

As of this moment, about a week later, it appears that it was the choke system on the carb that was the main culprit, that kept the engine flooded at low throttle, that led to the destruction of the starter, that was not fixed by spraying with OFF. Starter has been replaced, choke worked on, so maybe its fixed. We got about 75 pounds of shrimp for both of us.

June, 2005 Chandeleur Islands Sail

Dear Friends

These islands are south of Mississippi, but legend has it, when the offshore boundary between Mississippi and Louisiana needed to be determined, a barrel was pitched into the Pearl River, which bounds the states upstream, and floated out to sea. The path of the barrel became the boundary between the states. The barrel took a turn to the east upon exiting the mouth of the Pearl, therefore the Chandeleurs were blessed to become part of Louisiana.

You probably know this, the island-forming nature of big rivers like the Mississippi River, wherein turbulent waters carry lots of sediments to the mouth where the velocity drops as the waters spread out on reaching the ocean, the sediments then drop out, damming the river at the mouth. Then a big rain comes upriver, the dam at the mouth impedes the big flow, and the river then breaks out sideways way upstream somewhere and cuts a new course. Then there is a crescent shaped island where it used to empty into the ocean or gulf. There is such a situation here, which formed the Chandeleur islands, a part of LA actually, but straight south of MS, sort of SW of Biloxi. These islands are maybe 30 miles long, and 30 to 40 miles from the mainland.

From the MS coast, moving southward, you go about 12 to 15 miles and come to barrier islands, then go another 8-10 miles out and come to the N end of the Chandeleurs. They form a mild crescent, trending NE-SW. Last trip on Armordillo, (steel homemade sailboat, get it?) Sandra and I went there, took a day and a half to get there, and we made landfall about halfway along the crescent, on the inside. The outside is steep and pounding surf, whereas the inside is quite shallow, and we came to realize, treacherous. We stayed overnight, uneventful, anchored in about 6 feet of water, about 1.5 miles from the island. Next day, we wanted to approach the island, walk on it, so started cautiously trying to work our way in. Boat takes 3 feet, and we ran aground frequently, but managed to find channels about 4-5 feet deep to keep working our way inward. As we progressed with this, through much of the day, the wind picked up from the SW, pushing us toward the island. I eventually came to realize that these channels, which were almost parallel to the shoreline, were a trap, and with a wind as it was, we could be grounded and pushed into the end, lifted up wave by wave and dropped on ever more shallowing water. So, I got us turned away from land and tried to go straight out toward deep water, but there were sand ridges we could not cross.

Eventually, with some consternation and increasing winds, we had to motor miles back down the exact GPS path we followed in getting into this situation. This put us at about 3 pm in 15 kt winds, shallow water, and 3 ft waves.

We eventually got into deeper water, about 10 feet, and started heading on a run toward the N end of the chain, thinking we would round the tip and find protection for the night. Boat rolled around maddeningly for hours, finally got there about 6 pm, found that the island had extended itself in a long arch to the NW, so we kept probing to cross this bar, which took us some miles further afield from our anchorage. By and by we got around it, went back S trying to get out of the waves on the E side. However, the waves were rolling in there to, quite the mixed sea, which made it all the more aggravating, pitching and rolling at anchor. We wanted to go ashore, and did, in the dinghy, but found another bar off the beach, inside of which was another deep channel. I was not too pleased with leaving the boat anchored out there, jerking mightily against the anchor while we explored the beach, but that is what we did. Got back as it was getting dark, and pulled anchor and motored hither and yon in a little zone about a half mile long looking for the sweet spot. There was no sweet spot, and when I anchored finally it was apparent that it would be so rough we could hardly stay in the bunk.

As it got dark, we gave up on anchoring and headed N looking for the barrier islands, namely Ship Island, to round and anchor. Seas still big and rolling astern from the port quarter, boat so active it would wear you out just to try to sit in the cockpit. We had never been in this area before, and were trying to make the best of what showed up on the little GPS map program A maddening thing about this, that developed later in the night as we thought we were getting near the island, is the GPS has these warning notes that show up in a rectangular box on the screen. We were trying to find the W end of the island, which had no lights on it, and if it had we would not have known what to make of it anyway. When I went to large scale on the GPS, this warning notation about an ammo dump would override the mapping feature and obliterate the end of the island that we were trying to find. I would have to back off on the scale, go to small scale, where the boat symbol was probably a mile long, before the island came back on the screen. All this led to an ongoing uncertainty, and with the boat rolling so much the rails occasionally went under, and with the dingy surfing on the waves and slamming repeatedly into the transom, and not being able to find the island on the GPS, and the wind continuing to pick up, we were wondering whether we would have to keep up this fight till daylight, and whether we were going to find ourselves washed up on the seaward side of the island we were trying to round. The backlight on the GPS is no good, so every time I looked at it, I had to use a flashlight and then my night vision would be gone.

We rolled and pitched, and moved N. for hours, looking at the depth on the sonar, turning on the flashlight and trying to make out what we could on the small-scale GPS, and kept moving into the unknown. I finally intuited that we surely had to have passed the tip of the island, so we turned E and started trying to get behind it, all the while not knowing quite where it was. Eventually I decided that we had to be inside, although from the waves and wind you would never know it, so I decided to just head S, approaching I hoped the inside of the island that we could not see, and go till the depth got to 10 feet or so and anchor. Finally, all this paid off and we got into protected water 5 feet deep around midnight, got anchored, and had the rum celebration, hot and worn out.

Seems like a lot of consternation for a short little trip off the coast of Mississippi. I know you did not sail at night, and maybe I need to change something in that regard. This whole run day and night with the stern quartering waves was tiresome on the whole, and anxiety-producing in the dark wondering exactly what an ammo dump was, how deep it was, whether there were actually things to hit on the seafloor, and trying to find the island in the dark. I tend to ignore the weather and just roam around to new places, but Sandra is presenting a persuasive argument that we need to pay attention to the weather and have something more of a plan, and plot anchorages in advance, and get into the anchorage before dark. Most of our anchorages are something not obvious that we find as the day wears on, and some of them have been totally unsatisfactory. Most of the whole area this trip was in, way offshore, was still only 20 feet deep much of the time, 40 feet max, so if the conditions were moderate, one could just anchor out there in the open water.

Well, you asked for an account, and there you have it.

June 29, 2005 Bridge Calamity

Plan 1, which we have come to call it, was that Thursday I would sail E from here with Armordillo packed with the necessities of life, i.e., rum, wine, vegetables and ice, and sail over to Cat Island, which is off the SW coast of Mississippi, spend the night there, then sail into the harbor at Pass Christian to pick up Sandra about noon. She was to drive over on Friday and leave the car in the parking lot, and join me, for some sailing among the islands about 15 miles off the MS coast, known as the Gulf Islands National Seashore. The plan was that on Monday I would return her to the port, and then take a couple of days to sail back home.

Departed, sailboat under diesel power, at 0740, went through the two swing bridges, the car bridge and the train bridge which are right here at the start of any trip, turned E into the Intracoastal Waterway (ICW) and discovered that the wind was directly on the nose, i.e., blowing straight from the direction I wanted to go, so I planned to keep motoring in the ICW until I got to open water, then put her under sail for the remainder of the trip, which would involve long tacks in open water, about 5 mile legs each, till I raised Cat Island. Saw a couple of otters playing along the way.

Nearing open water, the engine started making a scraping sound, so I slowed down and looked into the cabin and discovered water spattered all over the aft flooring, with black deposits floating in puddles. Veered the boat over to the side of the channel, near a cut where I could get out into the bay if necessary, anchored, and went below to see what happened. The metal fitting on the engine which the exhaust hose fit over had corroded through, broke off, so all the exhaust and cooling water discharge was being pumped out over the top of the engine and spattered all about. This clearly put a damper on the plan. I called Sandra, first time in my life I ever needed a cell phone on the water, by the way, and told her not to go to Pass Christian, that I was going to sail out into the Bay and circle back toward home, and anchor off Alligator Point, a few miles from the swing bridges, and get Leron to come with his power boat and tow me through the bridges.

While sailing over, I decided that we could have an altered sailing vacation, no engine, if someone could bring Sandra out to the boat when I got off Alligator Point. Got all that done, and she joined me about 1730. With no engine, and no way to recharge the batteries, I decided we needed to move to a more out of the way spot where we could anchor for the night without an anchor light burning all night. Wind had died at this point, and it took us several hours to move about 3 miles. Anchored, had supper and what all, next day was a dead calm. Decided to cross the Bay (Lake Borgne, which is not a Lake in that it opens to the Gulf, so I call it a bay). Not a breath of air (wind) till about 1300, then we sailed across at a speed of about 1 knot (kt). Reached the other side at 1730, anchored etc. Next day, dead calm. Our Plan 2 was to have been to sail to some other islands near the offshore MS state line, then back home by Sunday afternoon. This dead calm problem eliminated that possibility, and since we were generally getting cooked in the heat, we decided plan 2 had to be scrapped, and we would just sail across the bay and into the river system and anchor near the bridges and get a tow through the bridges and on to home.

Started sailing across, which at this point was 6 nm (nautical miles) across, at a speed of 0.4 kts. At this speed it would take 15 hours just to reach the other side. Spent most of the day just inching forward, hot as hell, no wind to cool. Around early afternoon, some wind came up and we finally got across and into the river system about 1600 hrs. Sailed on in to a shallow point near the bridges and anchored.

At this point, here is some pertinent information relative to our situation. Lake Pontchartrain is connected to the outside water world by two deep and narrow rivers, the Rigolets, and Chef Menteur (Chef Pass). Chef Pass (the Chef) is where we were, and the currents rip through there, depth is 50 to 80 feet. Going home, the train bridge comes first, then about 400 yds on, is the car bridge, which is the crossing of the Chef by US Rt. 90. At the time we dropped anchor in shallow water along the edge of Chef Pass, the tide was strongly coming in, that is moving in the direction we had to go to get through, toward the bridge. We would be under tow, going with the current, and if the bridges did not open when needed, it would be tricky. But, with some situational awareness and good boatmanship, it would be reasonable to tow a 10,000-pound sailboat through, with the current, with a fishing boat powered by a 60 hp engine. To foreshadow, it would be an understatement to say that most everything conceivable went wrong, because some of what went wrong was beyond anyone's imagination.

I called Leron and asked him to come back out with his fishing boat and a polypropylene line (it floats) and tow us through the bridges. He was reluctant but agreed. I phoned another neighbor and asked him to come out with a bigger boat, so they both came out, Leron first. I called the train bridge operator while we were anchored and explained that shortly we would be under tow, pulling a sailboat through the bridge, and asked if there were any impediment to his opening for us when the time came. He said there would be no problem, he would be on VHF channel 13 ready to open whenever I called. I got Armordillo tied to Laron's boat Beluga (the fishing boat, and realize that little fishing boats often are not named, a key problem as it turned out in this saga). I asked Leron to pull us out into the current but to go into the current and to hold us against the current till we got the bridge open. I called the bridge and asked them to open just as the tow operation was getting under way.

Leron started pulling us at a very low speed across the current, instead of into it, and he was going so slow he had no steerage and neither did we. In the meantime, the bridge operator did not open the bridge, but started asking all these maddening questions about what was the name of our boat, what was the name of the tow boat. While I was talking to him and trying to get the bridge open, Leron still would not apply enough power to get control of our direction, and we were being swiftly swept by the current toward the bridge, which was about 200 yards away. I started yelling at Leron to give it some power and get us moving, but he claimed it would sink the stern of the tow boat if he did so. Instead he started this slow turn into the current, but would not give it enough power to move the sailboat, so the sailboat became a pivot point and Leron completely wrapped the tow rope around the sailboat. It was quite apparent at the beginning of this maneuver that it would be a disaster, but he did not see it and just kept on. By and by, the tow boat became snubbed up and entangled with the swim platform on the back of the sailboat, with Leron just sitting there with motor running at a slow speed forward, just the technique that created this situation, like somehow this situation would correct itself.

I had given the handheld radio Sandra to argue with the train bridge operator, and at the peak of this crisis, boats were wrapped around each other and swiftly moving toward being swept by the current under the bridge, which had about an 8-foot clearance, which would have probably sunk the sailboat and pulled the motorboat under. The bridge operator said he could not open the bridge till he got the name of the fishing boat that was doing the towing. Sandra told him it was Beluga, and some moments passed and the bridge did not start opening, and he came back and wanted to know how to spell it. Recall that I had explained all this to the bridge operator while we were anchored and he said he would open immediately when asked. It would be reasonable to conclude that he put three lives in danger with his hard-headed obstructionist lying to us.

The whole while this was going on, a rather large Sheriffs Dept Search and Rescue boat was idling against the current within 50 yards of us and did not do a thing to help. The only way someone could think we were not in trouble is to have no projection capability whatever.

I got onto the swim platform, then onto Beluga, told Leron to put the engine in neutral and quit pulling that way, and hand over hand pulled Beluga off the platform, back alongside the sailboat, got it pointed in the right direction for the tow, and yelled at Leron that he had to move out and put the power to it. He finally did so, did give it some power, and we started moving against the current and away from the bridge. Meanwhile, Sandra had continued her argument with the bridge operator, who was wanting her to spell "Beluga" for him as we drifted toward collision with the closed bridge.

That crisis was over, finally the bridge started opening. It was very slow. I realized that I was going to have to tell Leron exactly what to do every inch of the way, and started yelling instructions over the noise of the engine. Bridge open, tow boat applying power to give us steerage, we went into a big sweeping turn, got straightened out and aimed at the bridge opening, and went on through. 400 yards on was the car bridge, current and power sweeping us swiftly to an encounter with it, and they said they were opening. Leron just kept going at the closed bridge, yelled back at me asking if they were going to open and I yelled back that they were, so he just kept going straight at the closed bridge.

Leron and I have seen this bridge open many times, and it is maddeningly slow. 200 yds from the bridge it had not budged and Leron was still going straight for it. I started yelling for him to circle right, which he did, in a big arc, with power, the sailboat followed like a trained dog, and we got going the other way into the current, a holding position, while this bridge opened. This now was going so well I thought our troubles were over. Got Leron headed back with the current, toward the bridge opening, sailboat trailing along behind, but Leron did not aim for the middle of the opening, nor did he ever look back to see where the sailboat was. This opening is about 60 feet wide, he was a bit left of center, but the sailboat was being carried by wind and current off to the left and, projecting again, it was clear that the sailboat was going to slam port side into the bridge foundation. I started yelling for him to go right, and still oblivious to the problem, he thought I meant for him to go to the other side of the cribwork projecting out from the bridge pivot point, and started trying to do that, which was clearly impossible in that he was getting himself, us, and the towrope crossways to the current and we would then get hung up on the bridgework, him on the far side of it, us on the near side of it, pinned there by the tow rope and the current. More yelling and I got him back in the proper approach, off to the right side enough to pull us off the line of impact with the bridge foundation, and finally, we were in the clear, or so I thought. Incidentally, the car bridge had been out of commission for most of the day, repair crews were working on it the whole time, yellow rotating lights on numerous white repair trucks parked on the bridge. It was put back in commission and able to open for us no sooner than the moment we approached it. They did everything they could, unlike the train bridge, to remove the obstacle of the bridge opening, and I am not sure they were ready to open even as they did. It surely made some terrible grinding sounds as we passed through. We knew nothing about this till later, but wondered at the time what all the flashing yellow lights were about.

Tide was still coming in as we turned under tow into our canal system, and shortly were faced with a left turn into the canal where we lived. Leron did not start turning soon enough considering the current, did not give it enough power, did not look back to see what was happening to the sailboat, and entered the canal with little room to spare for himself, and, projecting again, put us on a path to slam starboard side into the pilings of a dilapidated dock there on the point. I started yelling again at him to give it the power, he did so, and pulled us away from impact with little room to spare. This put us in the canal, boats tethered to docks along both sides, and no way to slow down. So, I slipped the tow line and as our boat moved past our dock with considerable momentum, dropped anchor to stop it from going further.

Sandra has pointed out to me that recent past events on Leron's boat should have been sufficient for me to realize that we could have a serious situational awareness problem with the tow through the bridges. Also, Leron showed up to help, even though he had serious misgivings, and he is to be commended. He was scared, had been awake much of the previous two nights worrying about how we would handle the bridges, and was wearing a life preserver fully expecting Beluga to be sunk by these maneuvers. He has proven himself to be a true friend in this oblique manner, and that is a rare thing.

Had I been more cognizant of dealing with a situation that was new to those helping me, and realized that I was asking help from a person who simply did not have the makeup to contend with the vagaries, I never should have attempted a down-current tow under these circumstances, but should have just stayed at anchor, however long it took, for a stilled or mildly outgoing tide, which would make control of the tow safe and dependable. The actions of the train bridge operator were completely out of line. All the hassle about boat names is not in order, in fact, when the bridge opens, all manner of boats pass through without giving boat names. I have since filed a formal complaint with the US Coast Guard and CSX railroad about this, as such behavior endangers lives.

I simply did not foresee that it was possible to have such a dangerous mess develop in the situation described. The crux of the problem is that with a light tow boat and a heavy towed boat, when the light boat is tethered at the stern and tries to turn with insufficient power applied, the load from the towed boat keeps the stern of the tow boat from shifting in the turn, therefore the turn is prevented, so the tow boat pulls at the end of the tow rope and simply winds around the heavier boat till it is snubbed up against the heavy boat and rendered helpless. This situation does not develop quickly, you can see it happening, and the solution, right at the start of the effort, is to apply enough power to the tow boat to prevent this.

Followup: We learned about a week after this that on the day we were supposed to be at Ship Island, a savage storm swept through and wrecked–beached–nine boats, washed them ashore, on Ship Island. One was a 40-foot motor yacht.

June 30, 2005 Towing

Dear Hammond,

We thoroughly enjoyed your adventures. Regarding the towing, wonder if you have considered rafting the vessels together with suitable fenders using the sailboat rudder for steering and the motor boat engine for power? We have done it with outboard runabout as source of power. It is interesting to know of your successful shrimping in spite of carburetor trouble. Keep on telling us these sea stories for our vicarious pleasure! Best, Cas and Marina

>

Marina and Cas--Considering what happened, the rafting approach would have definitely been better. We considered it, and if we were to do this again, downstream, it would be my choice, notwithstanding the fact that people around here are drunk and oblivious on holidays and race with big wake right by rafted or towed boats without a clue as to what they are doing to others, and this would definitely play havoc with the two boats. I wanted to test the towing method before committing to the downstream approach to the bridge, and specifically asked Leron to turn into the current and pull us away from the bridge to get some space for testing.

This led to a tangle where the towing boat and line were wrapped around the sailboat. The sailboat had a 30-foot mast, and this tangle was being swept by a strong current toward a swing bridge closed to river traffic with about and 8-foot clearance. The two actions that led to this tangle were that he did not go into the current, but went across, and he did not apply enough power to the outboard to get us moving faster than the current, nor for anyone to gain steerage. I have felt rather stupid about this whole thing, wondering how this could have happened. Then I look out the window, and up the canal comes another impromptu towing operation, all kinds of boats pulling all kinds of boats, a rather frequent event, and I have never seen the sort of mess we had.

In the end, after pondering this thing continuously, and feeling the anger course through my bones and blood vessels every time I think of it, and blaming myself for putting both boats and three people at risk instead of just sitting out the tide for 3-5 hours till it turned, I come up with this: I expect a person who is a long term boat handler and shrimper to be alert, aware of what is happening, and competent. Just where this thing about sinking Beluga if power were used came from is a total mystery. I think Leron invented it in his imagination during the days Sandra and I were sailing around before coming back and asking for a tow. In a chat before we started the tow, he insisted that powering Beluga would force the stern underwater. That comment was such nonsense I failed to respond to it and thereby had to face it later in difficult circumstances.

Regards,
Hammond

2006-2007

January 10, 2006 Laughing Gas

Reading this book on the history of nearly everything I came upon a reference to laughing gas that reminded me of a post Katrina comical episode. The book mentioned that laughing gas when inhaled produces a comical trilling instead of speech.

I saw this guy sneaking around a house over by old Spanish trail and watched him for a while. It seemed he was a burglar looking for a way to get in. So, I called the cops and as this was still a time when the neighborhood was wrecked the New Orleans Police male and female and the National Guard showed up, several cars, one Jeep and probably 8 people.

Guns drawn they approached the house from all sides and started looking in doors and windows cautiously and eventually started knocking on the door and could not get a response. They kept this up for a while, knocking on the door, finally somebody came. There was a long verbal discourse. They dragged him out, handcuffed him, and walked him over to a squad car, put him in the back.

Eventually they took him out of the car, removed the handcuffs, and took him back into the house.

I went over to talk to them to see what had happened. They said when he came to the door that he wasn't making any sense and they can understand why I called the cops. He was taking laughing gas. So, his efforts to communicate with them would be described as a comical thrilling. They said taking laughing gas was not a crime so they let him go.

I have not called the cops or the National Guard about any potential burglaries since this happened. This whole message is Google Voice to Text so anything nuts about it is Google's fault.

February 5, 2017 Lost Hoodie

This concerns a hoodie that Wade left here before Hurricane Katrina. The storm waters washed it out of the house into the mud laden sludge that was up to the second floor at that time. Time passed and we obtained the sailboat Bes to replace Armordillo and put Bes up for sale. Bes was bought by Dr. P who wanted me to teach him to sail on a trip from here to Pensacola which he thought would take 8 days if we swung by Naples Florida on the way. He was asking about some peculiarities of the effect of the storm. I mentioned that this particular hoodie later was accidentally discovered under about 12 inches of soil in the front yard when we were planting some shrubbery. After quietly thinking this over for a while Dr P asked me what I would do if I discovered that the hoodie were lost again.

I told him that I would dig up the front yard looking for it.

October 4, 2007 Life on the Water

Guy--Water is up, has been for a week or so. That means that the dock is about one inch above the water level. I have been hearing about baiting shrimp for years, but never think of going to a feed store to get the lab rat food or fish meal or whatever bait is needed, and there aren't any feed stores around here anyway after the flood.

So, I decided to try the cheapest cat food, wondering if it would sink. Got a sack for about $3.50 from the new WD, turned on the dock light about dark, threw out some cat food, and it did sink, and went back out after dark, cast off the dock with the net, and in about 10 casts got around 40 or 50 live shrimp. That, supplemented with some dead shrimp which I have frozen in abundance, is enough for a good fishing trip. I can stockpile the live shrimp too, once I test my blue basket and see if they can swim through the mesh, or jump out the open top. This is the lazy approach, which avoids my having to build something for the shrimp, but it may come to that. Went out before daylight and got only about 5 shrimp and a flounder by casting the net off the dock, so no more this before daylight stuff, thank goodness.

If you aren't envious at this point, I have failed. These little projects, with the little details, and the little choices to be made, and the results to observe and the adjustments to make thereafter, and the messing around that continues to be necessary, keep a fellow going. Seeing as I don't have to make a living anymore, just keep living. This is a fine place for just keeping living. Course you are welcome to come see for yourself whenever you want.

2008

January 28, 2008 A Sort of Heritage

Through a carefully planned and executed plan that was planned and executed carefully we mainly I was responsible for failure to steadily save as other more responsible people did and furthermore due to some insecurity or wanderlust did not want to be tied down with owning a house therefore avoided the equity that would have accrued and put us into a self owned house much earlier and due to my desire to go up in grade and get more control over things put that first over building equity in some boondock or tax hell of a place and due to building a boat instead of buying a lot wound up gallivanting over the water instead of taking out a second and a third job and due to wanting to have a peaceful couple of cups of coffee of a morning every morning did not devote that daily hour to some profitable enterprise and due to investing in a mutual fund early on that steadily lost money for something like 7 years before I woke up and realized that the bastards were lying to me and just wanting to move the money here and there so they would get a commission each time and it was only 4K anyway but that was real money back then and could have amounted to more but I kept listening occasionally or more often to the self-important asses who proclaimed loudly in public why you implied dumbass your savings account not even earning enough to offset inflation so the stumbling around continued till recently and we now more set than before and not regretting much and glad the plan worked so much to your advantage and you and yo brother turned out to be so much like or improved over your progenitors.

Love,

Dad

Sure am glad you all didnt raise us filthy rich. Look at the dead Christian Brando at age 49 after his drug and alcohol rehab. Shot his sister's boyfriend in the head and killed him, served 5 yrs. in prison. The sister killed herself later in Tahiti. Christian a suspect in killing of Robert Blake's wife, his exgirl-friend. And now prematurely dead.

Love, Hammond the fourth

July 25, 2008 Venetian Isles Canal Debris

From: hammond eve <hamsan@bellsouth.net>
Sent: Friday, July 25, 2008 9:46 AM
To: Hadley, Edwin <; Richardson, II Leo F. >; duplessisa@legis.state.la.us; Fielkow Arnie <AFielkow@cityofno.com>; jdeberry@timespicayune.com; Willard-Lewis Cynthia <cwlewis@cityofno.com>
Subject: Venetian Isles Canal Debris

Lee, Eddie, Cynthia, Arnie

Yesterday I got in the canal (Canal 3) and walked/swam in the sludge from my boat to the mouth, going back and forth trying to find a route deep enough for my 5 foot draft boat to transit. Pre Katrina-this area was 8 feet deep. Now most of it toward the center is about 4-5 feet, changing to 3-4 feet near the mouth. Sides are well filled in from what they were pre-Katrina, now 1-2 ft deep. My neighbor across the canal operates a shrimp boat with just under 4 ft draft.

Right in the center of the mouth, the area that forms the chokepoint, I came across a mass of what I thought was barnacle encrusted sheet metal, stick-ing up about a foot above the mudline. Standing on this, water was just up to my hips. I hung around it in the water for about 15 minutes waiting to get someone's attention to throw me a marker. Eventually the shrimp boat

174

person, Martin Kain, showed up and found a board, which I jammed in the mud to mark the spot. Martin was extremely worried about his and his sons' boats which ply that area, so I offered to get some chain and rope and see if we could pull it out with his truck on land

Got the chain and rope, and dove down and found a way to work the chain around the debris at a constriction, and eventually got a pull set up to the truck. We pulled this piece out and found it to be a sizeable chunk of an above ground swimming pool. Removing that part exposed various pipes and hoses and valves with parts above the mudline, so I put chain on that and we pulled that up and on to shore. I then explored a bit further away from this spot and found a large curved pipe sticking up. Got the chain on that, pulled it out, and it turned out to be a galvanized steel 2-inch curved structure with a graduated scale on the base for turning, all bolted to a fiber glassed beam with large screws sticking out the bottom. Probing further underwater in the cavity that this removal created, I found more large barnacle encrusted pieces. Since the hole created was about a foot deep at this point, I jammed my arm in the hole up to the shoulder, trying to get to the underside of the remaining debris, which I believe to be a large part of the swimming pool. Could not reach the underside of it, therefore could not get a chain around it, but I doubt if we could have pulled it out anyway.

The government entities who are supposed to be helping with hurricane remediation have taken the position that this mud plug was not hurricane induced. This is a situation in which a swimming pool that was about 50 yds from this debris site is now under the mudline in 3 to 4 feet or water at the mouth of the canal, and extends to a depth below the mudline of at least four feet. That is as far into the mud as I could reach, and still did not reach the underside of it. This proves that this mud plug came after the pool came to rest in the bottom of the canal during the hurricane.

As to the health consideration, all this material had cutting edges and sharp points from screws, torn fiberglass, and barnacles. There are health hazards in dealing with it, and we citizens do not have adequate equipment for contending with it. As a consequence of my making the best of it and trying to clean up what should be a govt operation, I have lots of cuts on forearms and puncture wounds on most fingertips.

We homeowners have no equipment capable of getting under the buried swimming pool and pulling it out of the mud. Right now, the upper part of this pool is just inches under the mudline, the water is about 3 ft deep at low tide here, the big boats using the canal draw more water than this, and any of them getting a prop chopping into this pool will be damaged, with the ensuing commercial production lost.

I was on the coast guard boat with the side scan sonar looking for debris. Even though the metal and fiberglass parts extended above the mudline, nothing was detected in this area except mud.

This is years past the time of this storm, and this canal cleanup project seems to have died, killed by the bureaucratic people whose job it is to do this. The cleanup needs to start with firing some obstructionists and hiring some people with a different attitude, an attitude that seeks ways to do it rather than seeking excuses not to do it. This is the same situation as with building the replacement houses in Miss and LA. Miss has built thousands, Louisiana has built none, even though there are millions of dollars in govt aid for this purpose. Louisiana can't seem to get anything much done even when given money, due to indigenous incompetence, corruption, and a can't do/won't do attitude.

November 14, 2008 Seeking Clarity

Caught 20 keepers. I use the term loosely, but I did throw some back. Brought 20 home, cooked 20.

Took the Moons a school of 6 fried trout arranged properly on a plate, to their house. YM and I, eating at our house separately from the Moons, ate 9 trout. That leaves um, hell with it, some left over.

This was all about 6pm. I had several rums on the boat, 2 I think, and a couple more here, which sums up to a total of 2 for the day which I have decided is my limit.

I will try to be more precise in the future so stuff is clearer to all.
Love, Dad

Jacob Eve wrote:
Did he eat 9 trout or did he eat the trout AFTER 9 or did he and Mom collectively eat 9 trout or did he and Mom collectively eat 9 trout after 9pm?

December 20, 2008 Coyote

this morning at about 715 a large healthy coyote came trotting around the water side of Martins house, exploring yards and docks, crossed Hotard yard and dock, spent some time on Riedl dock and yard, went to Beverly's dock, got bewildered by the dead end on her dock, went back and forth for several minutes, looking up at the fence repeatedly, staring at it, finally jumped up and got balanced on the top edge, all four feet in the same spot on top of the fence, quite the balancing act, finally jumped into her yard, and continued this pattern all along the waterfront, every dock and yard, every bulkhead, till it came to the vacant lot down near alba east, where it went back toward the street.

I would rather have them than not have them. not that we have a choice. As a matter of history, mankind has been unable to contain the coyote.

2009

January 1, 2009 Antisatellite Hat

c

Sandra claims I am still under the influence this morning, but that is just nuts. I am sober as a New Orleans judge. But anyway, last night I brought out the antisatellite hat. The need is obvious, but I will explain it just to be sure.

We real men like to pee in the yard. I don't know why, that's just the way it is. But with satellite imagery, we can be spied on from space, and neighbors can subscribe to real time satellite images that zoom right in on what people are doing in their yard.

The antisatellite hat, picture enclosed, has a bill about 2 feet long, a dimension exactly calibrated for real men. Before going out to pee in the yard, install your antisatellite hat, bill squarely to the front, and level. Assume your stance and get going, but be sure not to turn your head. Most of us will therein be fully protected from aerial surveillance.

I don't know why my face is so splotched with red in the photo. Must be something wrong with the camera.
Happy New Year!!!!
Hammond

February 11, 2009 Sonic/Beauty/Cops

Sonic Saga

Some young males developed a specialty of robbing Sonic drive in restaurants. Their technique was to park a couple of blocks from the store, walk to the store, enter with guns, put all employees in the walk-in refrigerator, then take the money and go back to their vehicle and make their getaway. They were aware from watching the crap called news on TV that thugs were often on some camera somewhere and that the description used by police broadcasts usually related to a baseball cap and a T shirt with something or other printed on it. After selecting a Sonic in Slidell, LA, which is across the I-10 bridge from New Orleans, they took their getaway truck and parked it 2 blocks from the Sonic, leaving the key in the ignition, engine running, windows rolled down, so as to expedite the getaway. A Slidell cop wandered by, noticed the truck sitting their engine running, etc., so he decided to correct the problem. Turned the engine off, took the keys, locked the truck, and went about his business.

Robbery took place, thugs came running up to the truck, could not get in, did not have spare key. No cops around. From this situation, they decided to run to some woods and take off their clothes so they could not be identified. Got that done, left the clothes in the woods, and got back to the truck wearing their drawers. Had to break in the truck, so they pounded on the back windshield with some object and finally got it broken in, so they could get in, but still could not start the truck. In the meantime, the alarm had gone out about the robbery and the cops found them undressed in the cab of the truck with no key to start it

Beauty Queen Saga

This concerns the now deposed Miss Louisiana, I think it is an event that happened maybe 6 months ago. Beauty Queen, Miss LA, and four of her four-flushing female buddies figured they could eat in a nice restaurant and just walk out without paying and nothing would come of it. Just how much

180

of this they did was not reported. However, in this instance, they had their meal and walked out as planned, made their getaway without incident. Later, Miss LA discovered that she did not have her purse, and eventually recalled that she left it in the seat of her chair at the restaurant they had eaten at without paying. She went back to get it. By this time the restaurant management and the cops knew who they were looking for, and in she walked. No more Miss LA for her.

Future Events

There is so much beyond belief stuff going on here continuously that it just got the best of me and I gave up on reporting on it. For instance, not too long ago a New Orleans police officer was picked up in a marked city police car with light bar and all that stuff, driving around somewhere up there like Chicago, with a whore in the front seat with him. He and the car had been gone from New Orleans for several weeks and no one had made note of it or done anything. Chicago police eventually came to think a fully featured New Orleans police car that kept showing up on their streets might be strange and the NO cop got caught. What happened after that? Who knows, not me.

A young black man was sitting in a car at 3am in a crime ridden part of New Orleans with a 9mm Glock with extended magazine and extra magazines on the seat, waiting for his aunt or some other relative who was somewhere around, it was said. Somehow, a team of some 6 cops in civilian cars and civilian clothes got involved with this fellow, Grimes his name was, and shot him in the back 14 times. None of this Grimes thing makes any sense whatever, and the FBI is now involved, investigating Grimes and the cops.

There is a law limiting to about 60 the number of city owned vehicles used by city employees to and from work and on the "job", some driving to Baton Rouge where they live, every day. The city has about 270 of these cars issued to employees, many without records, all with city credit cards, all paid for and insured by the city, despite the law limiting the number to 60. Some employees were found to have two, and one was found to have four. Spouses and others were driving them.

The newly minted IG declared that if the mayor would obey the law it would save the city millions. The city council has tried to force the mayor to comply with the law by withholding some money from the budget. The mayor has essentially told the city council to get lost, that the law was outdated, and that, just to show he means business, he will order garbage collection reduced and street washing in the French Quarter ceased. The French Quarter, in case you have not been there, prior to this cleanup effort, smelled like a sewer and was so littered with trash and garbage on the sidewalks and in the streets, it was a hindrance to just walking, or breathing for that matter. Some savvy visitors would buy a pair of tennis shoes just for the French Quarter and throw them away after the festivities ended. The cop mess, the Grimes mess, the car mess, the garbage mess, is daily fodder for the citizen, a government not wanted by much of anyone, situations that no one wants, that we just can't get out from under. So many politicians in the wing turns out to be as crooked as the ones elected and reelected.

February 16, 2009 Excerpts of Office of Inspector General Report

"This investigation was initiated in 2006 based on allegations made by Chris Oynes, Regional Director, Gulf of Mexico Region (GOMR), Minerals Management Service (MMS), U.S. Department of the Interior (DOI), New Orleans. Oynes alleged that Donald C. Howard, Regional Supervisor, GOMR, had attended one or more hunting trips with officials of offshore oil and gas companies. The investigation disclosed that between August 2004 and July 2006, Howard accepted an offshore fishing trip, two hunting trips involving transportation on a company airplane, meals, and other gifts from Rowan Drilling Company, Inc. (Rowan), an offshore drilling contractor affected by MMS regulations and decisions. These gifts were valued at approximately $6,678. Howard failed to report at least one of these gifts as required on a Confidential Financial Disclosure Report (Form OGE-450) he submitted to MMS in October 2005. Subsequent to receiving these gifts, and at the apparent request of Rowan, Howard improperly issued a letter directing Rowan to salvage the Rowan Halifax, a Rowan-operated, offshore drilling rig that sank in the GOMR during Hurricane Rita in September 2005. At the time, this letter appeared to be integral to Rowan's efforts to collect $90 million in insurance proceeds related to the sinking of the Rowan Halifax and other Rowan drilling rigs. MMS terminated Howard's employment in January 2007 based on information provided to them by the OIG. On October 28, 2008, an information bill was filed against Howard in U.S. District Court for the Eastern District of Louisiana, charging him with one count of false statements (18 U.S.C. §1001). The charge stemmed from Howard's failure to report gifts he received from Rowan on the Form OGE-450 he submitted to MMS in October 2005. Howard pleaded guilty to the information on November 5, 2008. On February 3, 2009, Howard was sentenced to one year of probation. He was also ordered to pay a $3,000 fine and a $100 special assessment. In addition, he was ordered to perform 100 hours of community service at the "Rebuild Homeless Center" in New Orleans. Based on the above, no additional investigation will be conducted and this case will be closed."

February 24, 2009 Died Twice

Somewhere around 2003 we looked out at the main waterway and saw this fiberglass houseboat thing with an outboard motor anchored in the edge of Bayou Sauvage. A rather fat old fellow was casting a plug. Sandra somehow started a communication with them, across a distance of a couple hundred yards or so, and by and by they came to our dock and visited.

It was Tom and LeeAnn Hodges. He was an oilman, chemist, financial consultant with his own company, retired, and president of the Alabama chapter of the Sierra Club. She was retired nurse, retired CFO of their firm, member of Daughters of the King, a prayer group generally associated with the Episcopal Church.

He was in terrible physical condition and was hanging around waiting to be notified by Ochsner Medical Center about a heart for a heart transplant. Ochsner is about 35 miles from here.

Heart did not become available, time passed, Katrina came in 2005, we evacuated, and Tom and LeeAnn invited us to stay in their house near Mobile indefinitely.

He told me his whole medical history, a lonnnnggggg story, which included stents in legs, kidneys, heart, multiple heart bypass surgery, a ruptured aorta while he was in surgery requiring something like 29 pints of blood to keep him going. Much of this was before we met them.

I recently was kidding him about being smart, and he said he was smarter before he died. Since that made no sense, I pursued it and found that he was declared dead twice in association with the ruptured aorta.

So, I asked him if he saw the light.

Here is his response.
Date: Tue, 24 Feb 2009 07:11:20 -0600
From: Tom Hodges <tomhodges@charter.net>

Yes definitely. There were two angels and a very warm and very bright but soft light that it did not hurt my eyes. They came for me and I started to leave with them. It was a very pleasant experience, but we looked back and saw LeeAnn praying, saying, "Please don't take him!"

They turned loose of my hand and I went back to my body. That's why have absolutely no fear or concern about dying.

April 4, 2009, Contraption

The day started like any other day, fraught or not with potential, when Sandra and I decided it was time again to take action against the fat and walk for two miles and inspect the neighborhood garbage, excuse me, refuse, excuse me, goods offered to the public. Katrina cleanup and recovery still going on and people disposing of possible treasures, as John Burlett refers to this junk. Soon we came to a good prospect and upon examination found what appeared to be a genuine possible imitation of Murano glass, blue and clear, a vaaze, a thing to catch Sandra's eye. So, I collected it, and went next door to put it deep into a bricked up Katrina damaged snakes be damned mailbox for safekeeping to be collected as we passed back by.

There was a round, glass topped table, covered with Katrina mud, that we agreed was another good prospect, so I vowed to come collect it after our fat attack walk was concluded.

Remainder of trip was uneventful, and Sandra collected the imitation Murano vaaze from the possibly snake infested mailbox without consequence, and I got in the truck to go get the table.

Much to my dismay when I got back to collect the table, there seemed to be a property owner standing in the driveway. He gave me the glass topped table, but pointed out that buried under the pile was a galvanized steel contraption upon which was intended to be mounted a miter saw for cutting molding, and it had extensions that would extend, and underneath rollers that would roll, to make it all more expedient, for that purpose. I inspected it carefully and could not see how a miter saw could be mounted, therefore could not see how the extensions when extended would accomplish anything. It seemed just the right thing for me to collect, all galvanized, mind you.

So, I came back home with the loot, and spotted John Burletts pickup in his driveway, across from our house. Not knowing what to make of the contraption, but sure that it could be figured out if only a person were smart enough,

I decided to put it in the back of John's pickup without his knowledge, and did so.

Later the next day, after John spotted the contraption, and stared at it for a while, various other passersby came and the hung their arms over the sides and back of the pickup and stared at the contraption. Words were said that I could not hear. Every now and then, someone would stick their hand down into the pickup bed and do something, presumably move some part of the contraption, without resolution. It is still in his pickup some two weeks hence. I feel fulfilled, and highly satisfied in my efforts to accomplish something in retirement.,

Hammond

June 20, 2009 More Fish

Yesterday I was in the process of building another arbor as a screen to prevent the neighbors from getting their entertainment by watching us as usual, one to put a red passion flower vine on, when this 82 year old neighbor, Jim, came over and asked me to go fishing with him tomorrow, which would be today, and John decided to come too, as he was over here at the time wondering how many arbors it would take before Sandra was satisfied.

Last time I saw Jim he came over to ask me to change a bandage resultant from spinal surgery in the cervical area, and upon removing the old bandage, I looked into an open aperture and saw bones. Anyway, the three of us decided to go this am at 6 am. As usual I woke at 345 and was stuck with it, watched the sunrise, read the paper about more corruption in New Orleans and hoped and prayed that justice would be done, and made myself a magnificent breakfast, solo, as Sandra was in Waycross attending to her parents.

We got off eventually, and went by boat to a marina to buy some live shrimp for $55. Then it was a pounding trip out into the bay to the oyster bed. I had this new rig which was designed to lift the shrimp off the bottom by a few inches, thus preserving it for the trout, and avoiding the bottom feeders like catfish, stingrays and croakers. It was much admired by Jim and John, and Jim was ready to rush off an buy a bunch, but as the morning progressed, Jim and John were hauling them in and I was untangling the new rig.

The difference between theory and practice thus became apparent. The new rig had a shrimp on the hook on the end, followed by a small float about a foot back, followed by a heavy sinker about 2 feet back. In theory, the small float would lift the shrimp off the bottom by a foot or so and only the trout would get it. In practice, however, this rig must be cast, as in sailing through the air, and in doing so, the heavy sinker would take the lead, the float and shrimp would trail, and wrap around the line, and the whole thing would then plunge into the water in an ungodly mess, never to catch a fish. After a half hour of their catching lots and my catching nothing, I was ready to throw the dam thing ovahbode, as my father used to put it. Ovahbode is serious, final, never look back.

Switched to a rather unimpressive rig with a little bitty treble hook on it and started hauling them in. Pulled out from there about 10 am and came home with about 50 trout, some up to 3 pounds, as we weighed them with the scale Jake gave me. Then discovered that the water in the community was shut off.

US Rt. 90, the only road into this place, is lined with power lines and fire plugs, widely spaced. People are forever hitting one or the other, undoubtedly soused, any time of day, with good reason, which comes with living in this place. In this case it was the fire plug, which shut off the water supply for at least two days. The city has told us to boil the water, but we have no water to boil

So, I had this big pile of fish, and scooped up big buckets of salt water out of the canal to process them, and John came over to help and we took care of it, and gave a pile of fillets to Moon. I kept turning on the faucet to wash something, hands, plate, whatever, to no avail. That black cat, yellow reptilian eyes, got a whiff of the fish, came over, and I made the mistake of petting it as it demanded, and could not wash my hands. Being covered in sweat from the fishing, I felt awful and decided to wash in the salt water on the dock and swim around to get the soap off, right in the spot where I had just baited the alligators with all the fish scraps. Also, toilets don't work, can't wash the dishes or clothes, and the city is going to put some bottled water at the fire station for us to pick up tomorrow.

Clearly, alcohol was the solution to most of this trouble. So, I started in on that, and fried up a bunch of fillets and had a trout fillet supper, all I could eat, and everything got to be quite mellow, still is.

So, tomorrow i am going to Slidell to the fitness center we are evaluating, and take a shower. And there you have it, on the fringes of civilization.

Ham, New Orleans

June 29, 2009 The Trial of Judge Alan Green

I try to make my biases so obvious that you are not fooled, however, the facts are facts, and I think you can figure it out. There was no dispute about Green's taking money in envelopes, nor adjusting bonds, nor taking all kinds of largess, including trips, golf rounds, meals. Hard to dispute since it was filmed and recorded in various ways, and was so repetitive. The best the defense could do was spin it.

In that regard, we learn that Green was one of eleven siblings, and somewhere along the line one of his brothers had a runin with the law, went to jail, and, God Forbid, the bail was set too high for the family to get the poor boy out of the slammer. This bent Green forever after and he made it his mission in life to become a judge so he could set bonds that the poor people could afford so the criminals would be sure to get back on the streets. Contesting this nonsense, chief executive Lori Marcotte, of Bail Bonds Unlimited, sister of crooked and plea bargained bond king Louis Marcotte, testified that between her, Louis, and Alan, they cajoled to identify the entire family and friends of the perp and to figure out how much money they all could be milked for and to go after every cent they figured the family could gather, and then told Green what to set the bond for and he would do it. Furthermore, as demonstrated in the case of the rapper Corey Miller, as recorded in an FBI wiretap, Bowley, an executive with Bail Bonds, asked Green to set a high bond, and Green said how much, and Bowley said a million, and Green set it at a million five thousand.

Today's paper, the crusading Times Picayune, printed images from the videotape wherein Green was taking money, and there were more of these instances than we knew, and there was some racy stuff shown to make the corruption complete. There was the matter of Bowley handing Green the envelope with the $5000. But, in addition, a local lawyer was filmed, or videoed, handing over an envelope with eight one-hundred-dollar bills in it, and after the lawyer left, Green was seen taking three bills out, that would be $300, and putting it in his wallet. Turns out that this was supposed to be a campaign contribution to his niece who was running for state office. His niece's campaign managers said Green never gave them any of the money. Green said he gave it all to them. Niece declined to comment.

Another image has Lori standing in Green's chambers inches away from him, with his left hand on her right breast. This scene is located at the end of his desk, meaning he had to get up from his usual location behind his desk where he just reached forward to take bribes, as shown on videotape, and go half way to meet her for this little vignette. Now, this is a matter that the defense strenuously objected to, i.e., admitting this as part of the trial. But the FBI said it showed that Green felt that he had control over her and could do with her what he wanted, and the FBI view prevailed, so it was admitted. Lori said that she was there for illegitimate purposes in that she was bribing him, and what could she do in protest to his groping her?

They were having an odd conversation while this was going on, two totally unrelated sets of sentences. Green kept telling her he wanted to go to lunch with her tomorrow, and all her comments were about some case regarding a railroad, or railroading someone.

With regard to Green's accepting all these things of value, he dismissed it in his testimony by saying all judges do it as do various other govt officials, and that's just the way New Orleans is.

The jury has reached consensus on 5 of the 7 charges, but we don't yet know what the consensus is. They are deliberating now.

Don't worry, this stuff never ends, and the next corruption scandal is now under way, regarding the activities of the officers and others in the administration of the former mayor, Marc Morial.

Morial is now head of the Urban League, a national organization of black promotion, and his first act on assuming office was to start a program of blaming the plight of the black man on the actions of the white man and to try to produce statistics of various kinds to prove it, and to suggest that some more laws had to be passed to hand over wealth from white to black.

Four of Morial's cronies are now indicted. Just how his bosom buddy Stan "Pampy" Barre managed to enrich himself in this scheme is baffling, since he had no official position anywhere but seemed to exercise control over most everything. But as for the other three, it is quite clear. One was a city employee, top aide to Morial, who controlled the city purse strings. The other was an employee of Johnson Controls. JC was a contractor with an $81 million contract with the city. This second person, JC employee, was the one who submitted the bills that JC produced for the city to pay. The third fellow was a construction contractor and subcontractor to JC.

JC would produce a claim for the city to pay, and the JC liaison with the city, the JC employee, would add about $50,000 at a whack, to the bill. The Morial guy would pay the bill, and they, and at this point it is not clear what the full extent of the "they" is, would split the money. OR, alternately, the JC guy would submit a bill to the city, and the city guy would add a chunk and then write the check for the city to pay the JC guy, and they would split the money. The subcontractor to JC would do all sorts of construction work for this set of conspirators, on their private property, or buy things for them, such as a big barbecue grill, and bill it through JC, which would go to the JC liaison, which would then go to the city contact, to be paid. So, ultimately the taxpayer was buying all this stuff through this crooked chain involving JC. The FBI has stated that JC is a victim, not a conspirator. At the very least, hundreds of thousands of dollars were shifted from public to private hands this way.

The various charges are conspiracy to commit mail fraud, mail fraud, money laundering, obstruction of justice, extortion, lying to a federal agent. An attorney for one of the perps said "This is a poorly disguised attempt by the acting Republican U.S. attorney to indict and lynch the Marc Morial administration". A local attorney on the news last night opined that the ultimate target of the FBI was Morial, but the FBI apparently did not find him to be complicit.

The head of the FBI office put it this way, "This is not just stealing money, it is stealing the future"

And tomorrow, or whenever the verdict is out, we learn just how long Green will be in prison, one would think.

July 1, 2009 Chicken News
as reported by Times Picayune

Man with Local Ties Pleads Guilty in Frozen Chicken Plot
This has been clarified by the following elaborations:

man with New Orleans neckties pleads guilty while standing in a plot of frozen chicken.

man related to someone here pleads guilty in a chicken plot that got frozen.

Frozen chickens have plotted to tie man to guilty plea in New Orleans.

November 8, 2009 Dolphin Soccer

fishing been no good since we caught the 3. unusual, I guess if the tides get right the fishing will pick up again. suppose to be best time of year.

saw a bunch of dolphins doing what appeared to be something like a soccer game with a 4 lb flounder or some other fish that looked like that. pitch him up in the air, several feet, fish splashes back down sinks, then 50 yds away same thing, seems to be same fish but might not be, herd of dolphins engaged in this, swimming shoulder to shoulder in a phalanx going after this fish and pitching it out of the water.

November 10, 2009 Hurricane Hiatus

we are in good shape, thanks for the prayers.

water rose up about 4-5 feet, short of getting into our house, 18 inches in the clear. wind blew hard right down the canal from the north, sailboat roped across the canal to palm trees on either side. two foot high rollers smacked the boat in strong winds, reflected back almost the same size as hit the boat, and went back north against the incoming waves, each passing through the other intact. lines on the bow of the boat came to look like threads in the storm. green heron perched on one taunt bowline as it stretched like a rubber band, lifting him up, then letting him down where he was in range of spearing a fish, feet wrapped around the rope, struggling in the gusts that kept trying to turn him upside down, but, that's making a living. I guess some of us feel that way at times.

2010

February 27, 2010 A Frame
for Martin House

To: Guy Thurmond <guy@thurmondinc.com>

You can probably see how this works intuitively. However, just in case, the A must be about bisecting the rope angle when you first start the pull. It must be leaning toward the house so as to lift it up, but not too much so or it will just slide down to the post. you could roughly put it at about a 30 degree angle toward the house to get it started, and by the time the A is a bit past the vertical, you can just push it the rest of the way by hand. You can also secure the rope to the A with a couple of turns around the woodwork at the joint so it can't slide.

Have some big clamps or some such to secure it temporarily when it becomes vertical till you can get the bolts through. I am sure you would have figured this out without so much instruction, but better overdo it than leave something out. This seems clear enough so I don't expect questions.

April 6, 2010 Age?

I had a medical appointment today, and here is how it went:

Nurse: Sign your name and put the date.
Hammond: You think I know what the date is?
N: Its April 6.
H: Then what?

N: You must be retired.

The year is 2010, and

You are on Earth.

April 8, 2010 Danziger Bridge

The Shootings and the Start of the Conspiracy

In 2005, defendant HUNTER was an officer assigned to NOPD's Seventh District. On September 4, 2005, in the wake of Hurricane Katrina, the defendant and his fellow Seventh District officers were working out of a temporary station at the Crystal Palace on Chef Menteur Highway. In response to a radio call that officers on the I-10 high-rise bridge had taken fire, defendant HUNTER and other NOPD officers loaded into a large Budget rental truck, which HUNTER then drove from the Crystal Palace to the Danziger Bridge. En route to the Danziger Bridge, Sergeant A asked to borrow an assault rifle defendant HUNTER had placed in the cab of the Budget truck. HUNTER hesitated initially, but then relented and agreed to let Sergeant A use the assault rifle. When defendant HUNTER first observed the Danziger Bridge on September 4, 2005, he saw in the distance a handful of people casually walking on the roadway on the bridge. HUNTER realized that the people on the bridge would not know that the Budget truck held police officers who were responding to a call for assistance, so he used his left hand to fire warning shots, with his NOPD-issued handgun, out the window of the truck. As defendant HUNTER fired these warning shots, the people on the bridge scattered and ran toward a concrete barrier separating the roadway from a pedestrian walkway. The civilians, who did not appear to have any weapons, began to climb or jump over the barrier.

Defendant HUNTER stopped the Budget truck a short distance from where he had seen people climb over the concrete barrier. As the truck rolled to a stop, Sergeant A fired an assault rifle down toward the civilians on the walkway. At one point before HUNTER got out of the truck, he saw an older black male raise his head above the barrier, and he saw Sergeant A fire at the black male. The black male did not appear to have a weapon and did not threaten the officers. In addition to the people who jumped over the concrete barrier, defendant HUNTER saw civilians running westward, toward the top of the bridge. HUNTER got out on the driver's side, ran to the front of the truck, and fired his handgun in the direction of the people running away up the bridge. Sergeant B, who had also run to the front of the truck, stood nearby, firing an M4-type assault rifle at the same civilians. HUNTER did not see any weapons on these civilians, and did not see them stop or turn around. They did not appear to be a threat to the officers as they ran up the bridge. HUNTER fired his handgun numerous times in the direction of these fleeing civilians, but did not believe that he struck them.

Defendant HUNTER then walked to the passenger side of the truck, where Sergeant A and other officers were lined up in a position to fire at or behind the concrete barrier. HUNTER saw Sergeant A and one or more other officers firing at or behind the barrier. Seeing that there was no threat to the officers, defendant HUNTER shouted, "Cease fire! When the officers stopped firing, defendant HUNTER walked toward the back of the truck on the passenger side. While defendant HUNTER was still on the passenger side of the truck, near the walkway, he saw several civilians, who appeared to be unarmed, injured and subdued. Sergeant A suddenly leaned over the concrete barrier, held out his assault rifle, and, in a sweeping motion, fired repeatedly at the civilians lying wounded on the ground.

The civilians were not trying to escape and were not doing anything that could be perceived as a threat. Sergeant B and other officers started running up the bridge, as defendant HUNTER moved up the bridge to where two female civilians were lying on the walkway, behind the concrete barrier. The two females were lying on the ground, hugging each other and crying in apparent pain. HUNTER saw that at least one of the females had suffered serious gunshot wounds, and that both appeared terrified. One of the females had a gaping wound on her leg, and had a large chunk of flesh missing from her calf. The other civilians were also seriously wounded, including one man who was lying face-down, not moving. Defendant HUNTER did not see any weapons on or near any of the civilians when they were in the roadway, and he did not see any weapons on or near the civilians as they lay dead or wounded on the walkway. No officers on the east side of the bridge said that they had seen guns on or near the civilians after the shooting, and nobody asked the civilians where the guns were. At no time did any of the civilians make any statements about having fired at anyone.

Defendant HUNTER returned to the Budget truck, where he observed the assault rifle that Sergeant A had borrowed from him. The magazine that had started off fully-loaded was now empty, and the rifle was hot to the touch. Defendant HUNTER and Sergeant A entered the cab of the Budget truck and HUNTER drove to the crest of the bridge. On or near the crest of the bridge, they met Sergeant B, who said that civilians running toward the bottom of the west side of the bridge had fired at him. HUNTER saw three black males running down the bridge, but they did not appear to have weapons or to be a threat to the officers. Sergeant B may have fired an assault rifle at the fleeing civilians.

An unmarked car driven by an officer with the Louisiana State Police (LSP) approached from the east side and stopped near the crest of the bridge. Defendant HUNTER, Sergeant B, and Officer A entered the car. Sergeant B sat in the back seat, on the driver's side. Officer A sat in the front passenger seat. HUNTER sat behind Officer A. As the car moved down the bridge, defendant HUNTER saw three black males running away, near the bottom of the bridge. None of the civilians appeared to be armed or to be a threat to the officers. Two men, later identified as Lance and Ronald Madison, ran down the right side of the road, while a third, older man ran down the left side. As the LSP car drove down the bridge, defendant HUNTER focused on Lance Madison, who was wearing black clothing, and Ronald Madison, who was wearing a white t-shirt, with blood on it.

As Lance Madison ran toward the Friendly Inn, a motel at the bottom of the bridge, Ronald Madison trailed approximately 20 to 30 feet behind him. The LSP car moved to cut off Lance Madison and, in so doing, briefly pulled slightly ahead of Ronald Madison, who continued to run after his brother. As Ronald Madison then ran past the slowing LSP car, heading toward the motel, he passed by defendant HUNTER and defendant HUNTER had a clear view of him. Defendant HUNTER saw blood on Ronald Madison's shirt, and thought he might have been shot. Ronald Madison, who was running with his hands in view, had no weapon and posed no threat. Ronald Madison did not change his direction, turn around, or stop running as he passed the LSP car. Instead, Madison continued to run away, following his brother, who was a short distance ahead of him. At no time as Ronald Madison ran, did defendant HUNTER see him turn toward the officers, reach into his waistband, or make any threatening gestures.

As the unmarked LSP car pulled to a stop, Officer A, without warning, fired a shotgun at Ronald Madison's back as Madison ran away in the direction of the motel. Defendant HUNTER immediately got out of the car and went to where Ronald Madison was lying on the ground. Ronald Madison was alive, but appeared to be dying. He was lying on his side with two officers standing nearby. Neither defendant HUNTER nor either of the other officers searched Ronald Madison for a weapon. As Ronald Madison lay dying on the pavement, Sergeant A ran down the bridge toward Ronald and asked an officer if Ronald was "one of them." When the officer replied in the affirmative, Sergeant A began kicking or stomping Ronald Madison repeatedly with his foot. Sergeant A appeared to be striking Madison's torso with as much force as he could muster. Defendant HUNTER charged toward Sergeant A, who backed off from Madison. As defendant HUNTER walked away, an officer standing nearby appeared shocked that HUNTER had confronted Sergeant A. Shortly thereafter, Sergeant A approached defendant HUNTER and apologized for being "out of line." Sergeant A then asked HUNTER if HUNTER "[had] a problem" with the shooting on the east side of the Danziger Bridge. While on the west side of the Danziger Bridge, defendant

HUNTER heard Lance Madison ask the officers why they had been shooting at him and his brother. Lance Madison never said that he or his brother had possessed a gun or had fired at police, and Lance Madison did not have a gun in his possession.

HUNTER knew without question that the shootings he saw on the bridge were "bad shoots," meaning that they were legally unjustified. HUNTER later heard that the civilian, Ronald Madison, was a 40-year-old severely disabled man. Later that day, back at the Crystal Palace, defendant HUNTER met with the sergeant assigned to investigate the case (the Investigator), along with a lieutenant and other NOPD officers who had been in the Budget truck on the Danziger Bridge. During a roundtable discussion of the shootings on the Danziger Bridge, defendant HUNTER admitted that he had fired his weapon many times on the bridge. During this meeting, the lieutenant turned to an officer next to him and said something to the effect of, we don't want this to look like a massacre. All this was reported in the Times Picayune.

April 30, 2010 Life in the Crosshairs

From: Sandra Eve <hamsan@bellsouth.net>
Subject: oil spill and life in the crosshairs in Louisiana

Dear Family and friends,

This is truly a disaster on many fronts- beginning with the lives lost in the initial explosion and all families affected, and those economically dependent on these waters and estuaries. Please pray with us that God will intervene and have mercy with the weather, wind and tides and give wisdom, technical ability and safety to those in the forefront of the clean up to soften this terrible blow to so much of life in the sea and Coastal areas from Louisiana to Florida panhandle. The far-reaching effects of all this are too sad to pursue right now. It would be a sad day indeed if Zach and Ethan and you all could not visit here and expect to see a dolphin, birds, a playful otter, catch crabs and fish etc.... The nesting season is at its height in the marshes for birds, turtles etc. and not to mention how the marshes sustain the shrimp and crab reproduction. I saw a crabber and his helper leave an hour ago, hopefully to get to all his traps once more before the oil slick does. Multiply that scene by the thousands of crabbers, shrimpers, oysterers and fisher men . The livelihood of many, many people and animals is at stake . Thank you for your prayers, Love, mom/Sandra/Mamais'/Sandy

Hammond and Sandra Eve

June 18, 2010 Post Katrina Newshounds

OK mister, you wanted a report.

I have been called by reporters from all over the USA for about 6 weeks, and one thing stands out that stood in my craw ever since retirement. After giving a speech about a month before retirement, some in the audience said it should be written up and published as it was the best comprehensive explanation of the interplay of various laws affecting offshore oil and gas operations that they had heard. Running this up the chain to see what MMS desired, I was told by the top guy, "no one is interested in the opinions of an ex government official". Well hail fire, the wheels have turned, and that guy got fired, and no one is interested in the opinions of the current and ex officials who normally would be responding to the media, for the media are talking to me, not they. And, everything I have told them is popping out in the media across the USA, coast to coast. Could be that others are saying the same thing, or not, don't know, but the message is getting out. Also, this info is going into the congressional investigative committees, namely Nick Rahall (WV), chair of the house committee on natural resources or something like.

Had a 2-hour interview with a different NY times reporter yesterday, probably will have another tomorrow, and he may come to this house next week. One hour with Denver post on one occasion, shorter with another Denver post reporter on another occasion, some with Washington post. from that, other papers are picking it up, such as Portland Oregon paper, and it is showing up on internet blogs as if I had been interviewed by the reporter, even though I had not. I don't know how it is getting around, but it is as if they are cooperating with each other on the news, but i know that is not the case as they are quite jealous and protective of their sources.

A woman and her camera man showed up, making a documentary for French public television. We all sat on the back upper deck, rain drifting in, for hours during which she asked questions, they filmed and recorded my answers, and filmed various awards. After that specific interaction, she asked me to just talk on and on about anything so they could film me talking, nothing being recorded, for the final production. She said they would hire someone to talk over my commentary with a version in French, and the filming of my just talking would be used is if I were speaking French. I guess we don't want any lip readers in the audience. She said they used to use Gérard Xavier Marcel Depardieu, but he had turned into such a drunk they might have to find someone else. A government official from Guam called to find out if Tabasco sauce production would be curtailed.;

The new interior secretary, Ken Salazar, has decreed splitting MMS into 2 separate agencies, and abolishing the existing MMS, and if he does not partition it right, and does not eliminate some of the organizational structure messes that brought down the old MMS, it won't matter. Thus, the old ex govt official whose opinion was viewed as irrelevant is one of the few trusted sources of information from the media perspective and congressional perspective, and whatever comes of these interviews is presented by the most influential newspapers in the United States.

Now for the important stuff.

The oil spill is about 30 to 40 miles from here, proceeding east and west, not north, carried by currents and gulf eddies. Fishing is good, although i have not been going. Freezer thawed and we lost about 150 trout, 20 flounders, 30 pounds of shrimp and various other things. Huge stench, fight the stench every day, bleach, pine sol, finally yesterday it smelled like a low rent fetid public urinal, but after 5 gallons of bleach water yesterday, have about got it whipped.

Sandra went to Waycross GA to tend to her ailing mother, so she is now the 3500 mile woman, driving that far back and forth alone in several trips.

Am back from California, after helping Jake with a patio cover, and after gaining 5 pounds. This eating thing is maddening. Here i am trying to get rid of the 5, and about 20 more, and the food just keeps showing up. John brought over about 6 nice trout, so i fried them up and he and i ate them all yesterday, along with some roast corn that was so tough only an animal would eat it, so what does that say for John and me, huh?. Jim left a container of shrimp chowder on the inside steps yesterday, set off the motion detector alarm while i was on the 2 hour interview with NYT, and he just kept fidgeting around in front of the alarm, so the alarm would not shut up, and i could not concentrate on the future of the nation and the seafood supply and how to organize 3 new branches of government.

Also, i bought a half cooler of shrimp from John, about 30 count, ie, 30 to the pound, for 40 bucks, and was processing them yesterday am.

Finished the boathouse, got the hoist winches installed. Old bimini top on the boat tore up in a windstorm while the boat was on land, so i cut up the aluminum struts, and John gave me one of the banners that are put on big buildings for advertising, like the superdome, a fiberglass/vinyl fabric, bigger than my dock, and i proceeded to make another bimini out of that stuff, welding the aluminum with a 110 volt welder that was totally inadequate. Upper welds are inside the fabric, which is glued on with contact glue and cannot be undone without tearing the whole dam thing up again. Then, in more winds that whip around this house with considerable violence, the welds started breaking, so I sold my arc welder and the 110 v mig welder on craigslist and got a 240 volt mig welder and aluminum spoolgun and argon gas and went after repairing the welds I could get to on the bimini top, which amounts to rewelding the exposed lower welds and doing nothing with the

201

upper welds i could not get to cause of the fabric. Took er out on the water for a test run, hit a repetitive bunch of 1 foot waves that got the top whipping back and forth in a harmonic that I know will tear it up in the near future, so I am back this afternoon trying to figure out how to put some cross straps on it and still be able to fish out of the boat.

For this intellectual endeavor, realizing that it might not turn into actual physical work today, Ritchie is bringing over some rum and orange juice, and other stuff, and the rum and orange juice have plenty of calories, but a crisis is a crisis, and desperate measures are needed for desperate times, so I guess it will be tomorrow that I get more disciplined and start cutting off the weight, but, something is bound to happen tomorrow to undo this plan too. Johns son was to bring a bigger boat around this afternoon to go out to a rig fishing, the 4 of us, Ritchie, John, Elliott and me, which conflicts with the rum fueled bimini contemplation plan, but Ritchie could not find any croakers for bait for big trout, so the fishing plan becomes less attractive and leads to opting for the rum plan, but if 4 of us contemplate the bimini fueled by the rum... I wonder how this is going to be resolved?

So, Guy Thurmond, here is your report.

Hammond

July 10, 2010 The New York Times

Followup to 7/9
From: Hammond Eve
To: Jason DeParle, New York Times

Can a lease sale be stymied due to an EA or EIS that is flawed, you ask? If the EIS does not adequately portray the environmental impacts, for instance, leaves out some major consideration, an outside group can sue and if successful get a court order to fix the EIS before the sale proceeds. I believe this very thing happened a few years after I left. If this is a point of interest for you, I can try an internet search and try to find out more, or you can. Might enter something like--court blocks lease sale in gulf. On the nuclear power plant licensing an outside group did this, saying that the EIS must consider a terrorist attack, the court ruled otherwise, and the EIS was deemed OK. But, had it gone the other way, the court would have required fixing the EIS before the matter could proceed.

Clarification on MMS willingness to place environmental protection or remediation requirements on industry:

The environmental side was successful, not because of clout, or powerful persuasion, but because conflict resolution was cheap, relatively speaking. If you dropped 10,000 golf balls randomly into the Gulf of Mexico, odds are that not a one of them would land on the seafloor on any site of high biological diversity. Most of the biological diversity is swimming around, therefore, site selection for seafloor disturbance is rarely an issue. In the few instances where it is an issue, the solution is to move the template over a bit, or put the anchor or pipeline somewhere else, maybe only a few hundred yards.

The environmental requirements are along the lines of--relocate something, or reduce some engine emissions, or do a sidescan sonar on the seafloor, or a video, or take some benthic samples, or require a trained marine mammal observer on seismic boats.

For engineering safeguards, it is an entirely different matter, and MMS has shown that it is loath to do anything to increase the cost of doing business in the Gulf, and is quite willing to put the environment at risk to save the industry some money. The news coverage of the current disaster has been more informative on this MMS mindset than was apparent when I was working there. For example, the matter of not writing regulations that require improved blowout preventers did not make news nor stir ire within the environmental side because it was not within our province, as defined by MMS management, to be doing risk analysis on mechanical failures. However, some unbiased party should be doing exactly that, and the outcome should be factored back into the system and lead to changing engineering requirements on any mechanical apparatus whose failure could lead to significant environmental impacts.

And, mechanical failures throughout the world should be the data base to work from, not just what has happened recently in the Gulf in US waters. The goal must be to prevent the disaster, meaning that decisive action must be taken in advance. This gets right at the MMS mindset dilemma, requiring a change in equipment or process that costs millions of dollars for safeguards that the industry will say is unnecessary and wasteful, not to mention slowing everything down and increasing the cost of gas for cars.

Well, Sandra says I must go eat my fish and grits and tomatoes breakfast. I am not sure I am finished with this, ...

Hammond

2011

February 5, 2011 For Women Only

It is very exasperating when WOMEN start offering opinions on MECHANICAL THINGS, which is clearly the GOD-ORDAINED province of MEN. On rare occasions, GOD decides to let them be RIGHT, just to keep us from becoming INSUFFERABLE. It remains OUR GOD-ORDAINED RESPONSIBILITY to fight for ORDER and keep on with our QUEST to remain KING of MECHANICAL THINGS or else they (THE WOMEN) will take over and we will just walk about with our head hanging in SHAME and the women will wonder where the REAL MEN are and why they don't have one when the whole thing is THEIR FAULT for messing with the GOD-ORDAINED order and therein they PUNISH THEMSELVES for being RIGHT about MECHANICAL THINGS so it is in the best interest of the WOMEN to LET THE REAL MEN MUCK IT UP ON THEIR OWN WITHOUT ANY WOMAN"S COMMENTARY.

Blessings,
Hammond

February 14, 2011 Fin Keel versus Full Keel

what to worry about--
Fin keel hit something, worry about that.
Full keel hit something, hell with it, nothing will happen.

205

My steel, homemade boat, Armordillo, had a 3/16 inch steel plate, square, as the bottom of the keel, poured with concrete and steel machine punchings.

In Chesapeake bay, Bloody Point light, which looked like a giant bowling pin, used to sit there at a tilt with no rocks around, and i would sail right close to it to see if there were any fish on the sonar. Without my consent or knowledge, the Corps of Engineers went an put 3 ft boulders all around it, but below the water so you could not see them. They were about 2 ft below the surface. I was sailing Armor alone, on a strong broad reach, and pulled my usual sonar recon looking for fish, waves about 2-3 feet high, sailing fast with immense power, and slammed right into one of those rocks. It made such a horrible sound, jolted the boat, I looked around trying to figure out what had happened. Boat came to a standstill. Waves lifted her up, she moved forward, got past midships, hanging on the rock, tilted forward, slid off with a screeching rending sound, the wind got a grip on her again and off we went. Sailed her into shallow water, anchored, got a drink, waited for her to sink. Nothing happened. No water in the boat. Sailed her back across the bay to home, got in the water, hard pressed to find any damage whatever. Eventually found a dent in the keel about 1/2-inch-deep, 2 inches long. These heavy full keel fiberglass or steel boats are not going to suffer from a grounding even if it is on a reef.

Mike Plant, years ago, round the world racer, came into Chesapeake Bay with a high-tech fin keel racer, and it was said that he grounded at one point. Later he took the boat in the round the world, in a race I think, boat found upside down, Mike missing presumed dead. That is what happens when a fin keel boat grounds hard, it puts intolerable pressures on the hull or trunk and is dangerous as a design. But it turns on a dime, and goes upwind at incredible angles, but it does not track straight and has to be vigorously tended by hand or mechanical means. Worry about that, which is what you will not have.

H.

June 9, 2011 Life in The Fast Lane

on Thursday, Jim, our across the street neighbor, 85 yrs old. walked out into his driveway and got the paper, unbeknownst to him at the time, the Saturday paper, which had been laying there undiscovered since....Saturday.

Therefore, for Jim, Thursday was Saturday.

Sunday would therefore be tomorrow, and there would be church, and the neighborhood crawfish boil.

On Friday, midday, Jim showed up on our back patio all dressed up, asking if we were going to the crawfish boil.

I inquired as to why he was all dressed up like he was going to church, and he said he had been to church. now he was ready for the crawfish boil, were we going? I told him the crawfish thing was on Sunday. He told me today was Sunday, had to be, cause the Saturday paper came yesterday and he went to church today and he was going to the boil this afternoon.

He is catholic, so they have church every day or something, anyway, they had it on Friday and he went thinking it was Sunday. worked out ok for him.

I finally convinced him that today was Friday, and he pretty near convinced me today was Sunday. He wondered why so few people were in church on Sunday, anyway.

I am sure today is either Monday or Wednesday. Doesn't make much dif for we retirees, anyway, except for when it is Sunday, and if Sunday were not involved, I just don't know how long this could go on.

June 16, 2011 Retirement Plan

here is my plan. also, my counterpart to Bob Mistak's explanation of how time flies when you are retired and you spend days carving a baby wooden duck and have to go buy wood and knives etc for that duck even though you don't need them. In fact, don't need the duck, nor the knives, nor the wood, it's just a retirement thing.

pick the crabs that we cooked about 5 days ago, defer the huge batch i cooked yesterday. shell a big bunch of shrimp I boiled yesterday. ride the bicycle 7.5 miles. Mow the lawn on a riding mower. water the tomatoes. Put sevin on Johns crummy stink bug infested tomato row.

Friends coming over at 4 pm to eat some seafood and drink some beer. PhD anthropologist who did a dissertation on Alaska eskimos, a tome about 4 inches thick that i have been reading on for several months, and his Russian speaking wife. Remember that Russia is right next to Alaska, according to Palin, so this makes sense. They have to leave by 6 cause we are going to eat a steak special in town with the old goat Jim Roos and the other goat John Burlett, who gave me a bushel of crabs yesterday morning, and 3 flounder the day before, which consumed about half a day in the processing thereof, then the boiling of 5 batches of shrimp.

Accomplishments so far today. 3 cups of coffee and two tomato sandwiches that had a pile of vine ripened tomatoes stacked an inch thick with ground pepper and mayonnaise on oat bread. Gave away a batch of tomatoes to two neighbors.

Any suggestions as to how to improve this plan will be welcomed.

June 19, 2011 Politically Correct

Stewardess has ceased to be a politically correct word. Heaven forbid that anyone should utter such a word, much less admit in writing to even knowing it. And, there is no one providing service in public to the passengers who looks remotely like the figure in this message. The PC police are everywhere, and i can show you my tin badge on request. PC trumps every other consideration in this society at this time, so i am a very important person with my tin badge. My job is to look for PC transgressions and publicly brand every person with the scarlet P who is caught, and this is more important than national security. You may be the organizational genius who is well able to take the country out of its financial and moral and hedonistic morass, but one PC error and it goes worldwide immediately and you are past tense. I and my tin badge are the virtues of the future, even though it takes us fast down the road to Islam, poverty and disparity. You may subscribe to further inspirational and informative factual messages by giving me your credit card numbers and passwords.

2012

January 1, 2012 Not a Plant

c

These humongous jelly masses show up on salt and freshwater structures, to the dismay and mystification of observers. This is what they are, sort of brown from what i have seen. Harmless.

The Bryozoa, also known as Ectoprocta or commonly as moss animals, are a phylum of aquatic invertebrate animals. Typically, about 0.5 millimetres (0.020 in) long, they are filter feeders that sieve food particles out of the water using a retractable lophophore, a "crown" of tentacles lined with cilia. Most marine species live in tropical waters, but a few occur in oceanic trenches, and others are found in polar waters. One class lives only in a variety of freshwater environments, and a few members of a mostly marine class prefer brackish water. Over 4,000 living species are known. One genus is solitary and the rest colonial.

The things call seaweed, which are crusty filaments that wash up on shore, in different colors, like yellow or orange, and can be dried and used as decorations, are animals like the stuff above. But, the seaweed variety has a mineral shell, like a tiny barnacle, which it operates from, extending tentacles and sweeping in microscopic foods which it digests. It is a colonial animal, meaning that the whole is more than the accumulation of the parts in that each one operates for its own needs but contributes to the colony also.

February 28, 2012 Shock

(YM is yo mamma, Sandra Eve

just a short while ago, I saw a package on kitchen counter, already opened so thought your Dad had opened a package addressed to me. Proceeded to open lid and saw this skinned something lying there and almost had a heart attack in about the split second it took to realize it was a dead, skinned duck! did not scream, but felt the adrenaline and a choking sensation; found your Dad in his shop, laughing so hard he was shaking. The culprit, guilty as sin, almost made me have heart failure. So guess this person will try for first time in many years to cook a wild duck; the last one was on Winter street.. and you both and Wade in heaven know that story! "Fellas, YOU shouldn't have....

give me that duck!"

lm

August 30, 2012 Storm

Dear Friends and Family

The storm center has moved on but winds still sent floodwaters into Slidell, flooding old parts of the city, and the southern part of the city, and the roads we need to traverse to get back home. No flooding where we are right now, same place with friends.

Water in the streets in Venetian Isles as of a few hours ago was 3 ft deep, which is down and out of our house, but too deep to gain access to our house. Might be able to leave the truck on the highway and walk in if the water on the highway ever lowers. I expect to get in tomorrow. Still no power there.

Damage to our house so far, soffit on front deck off in part. shop garage and double doors out, water 2 feet deep inside but drained out now, leaving mud 2 inches deep throughout, possible minor roof damage, maybe spoiled food in three freezer/fridge (reefers).

Lots of rescues going on, some here in Slidell. hundreds of people rescued. Some levee breaches putting water to the ceiling in houses, a dam breaking upriver threatening about 50 K additional people. Communications on and off regarding internet and phone service. we will probably keep coming back to Slidell at night to get cleaned up and sleep till we get power back at home. Yargers have been very patient and generous hosts. one more hurricane and we will probably know how to play canasta.

Blessings
Hammond and Sandra Eve

2013

July 3, 2013 Confusing

Newspaper Header:

Police Rescue Pig Wearing Sweatpants from Hot Car

Were the police wearing sweatpants, or the pig. Or, does this call the police a pig and the police rescued another police, or in other words, pigs rescued a pig, and one of them was wearing sweatpants. Was a cop wearing sweatpants in the car and got rescued, or was it a pig wearing sweatpants that got rescued by the pigs, or were the rescuers wearing the sweatpants, or was it really pigs rescuing, and the author used the vernacular in reverse and called the pigs police.

Please clarify. also

Reformed anti-abortion foes lose.
I'm pretty sure I thought it was true.

August 20, 2013 Exciting Bummer

Not catching a dam thing. Shrimp are gone, so shrimpers are not going out. Ystd went for a bit and hooked some thing so big it just slowly swam away. i could feel every slow swish of its tail as an inexorable pull on the line and rod just slowly taking the line, pulling against the drag, till i saw the spool on the reel being bared, knew it was about to play out of line, about 50 yards, so started holding back on the spool trying to turn the fish before the line was completely out, pressure was insufficient to turn him, pulled to the end of the line, popped the line. 30 lb test. Must have been a shark. I doubt he knew he was hooked. whatever it was would be something i did not want. however, i do like to get a glimpse so there is no mystery about it. Thing about salt water fishing, is there are mysteries on occasion. We all seem to like that aspect of it. You can never be totally sure what is down there.

2014

April 12, 2014 Problems with the Outboard Motor

Motor would shut off on idle, which means it would not start at an idle and could not be shifted into gear without shutting off. Changed all filters, internal and external. Just like college days, put various additives in the fuel. Changed spark plugs, did compression test, shocked myself 4 times on each of the 4 cylinders to determine spark, with motor running pulled off each spark plug wire, shocking myself 4 more times, to ascertain that each cylinder was firing and powering. Took the fuel filter apart, a part that appears to cost $585, to the extent that it could be disassembled, which wasn't much of an extent. Replaced the squeeze bulb in the fuel line. At breakfast yesterday, Sandra, in the course of asking the blessing, asked God to give me a hand with this problem.

During the day it was mess with the motor as stated above. People can see me doing this, Joe from across the canal, and John from this perch outside his garage across the street, where he sits to watch what is happening in the street and both of them keep an eye on what i am doing. Before long, Joe and John were here, Joe bringing another fuel additive.

They watched me try various things to no avail. Fuel additive solution did not kick in at this point. John was watching me start the engine with throttle advanced and out of gear, then watched it shut off when i put it into neutral. He decided that there was some problem in the controls on the console, not with the motor, something like the kill switch, or dead man switch, getting

217

involved somehow and shutting the engine off every time i put it in neutral. He told me to jam the gear handle back and forth hard, repeatedly, to the full extent of movement, which i did. After that, engine started in neutral, everything worked. Still works. Motor back to normal.

I told John that he had a direct connection to God. He got all red faced and said something like "wha" "wha". I had to repeat it a couple of time. John looked all around to see if anyone were watching. Only Joe, who did not know what to make of this. I explained to John about Sandra's prayer and told him that God sent him over here to tell me to crank that handle back and forth to fix the motor. He stayed red faced and looking around to see if anyone were watching. Finally, he wanted to do the high five thing and go home.

I am going to cook a large chunk of pig, 10 lbs, all day, shoulder, and see how it goes. Come on over and let's eat it.

Hammond

May 8, 2014 Nano and Cats

Nanomanufacturing includes integration of topdown processes and increasingly complex bottom up or self-assembly processes.

If this means anything to anybody just keep it to yourselves.

Cats paw around in poop, put dirt over it, then prance around on your countertops, tails straight up, like they own the world, and if you are fast enough to slap them, they don't learn a thing except to move faster. They think they have won, the self-important little snits.

October 17, 2014 3 Days on the Waterfront

Day 1. Jake showed up Tues at 11 am, had to fly out leaving here at 4 pm, same day. 5 hours to do something.

So, ate fried oysters and shrimp at 11 am, then went fishing, Sandra, Jake, Me. Wind had been blowing 30 knots, dropped off a bit to 15 to 20 when we went out, water muddy, laden with detritus that hung on the lines like fine threads. License for Jake cost $20. Jake caught one small catfish, now referred to as the $20 catfish. S and I caught nothing. Bummer, but saw gator about 10 ft long just off the side of the boat about 20 or 30 so feet. Came in, took Jake to airport.

As I had been having some winch problems on the boat hoist, which uses two, one forward, one aft, decided to buy one from harbor freight on the way back from the airport, 5000 lb lift capacity.

Day 2. Decided to try the fishing again as it was calm, tried to lower the boat, main winch seized, boat dangling in the air in the boathouse. Would not lower. Spent the rest of the day making temporary load bearing ropes to catch the boat when it dropped upon my cutting the cable with a bolt cutter, then fabricating, cutting angle steel, drilling, welding, new mounting bracket for new winch, getting the old one down, the new one up, all quite heavy, took all day, required a three-shot rum prescription as recovery protocol.

Day 3. Went fishing finally, got nothing where we went on day one. then to Thomas Bayou, 40 ft deep, got some drum and a huge redfish. Redfish questionable as to eating it. I am inclined to not catch these things, but we did try it. Sandra marinated and baked a big slab of it. Still not our favorite, but we ate it, her prep saving the day.

Different from living in town, or on a farm. The situations have demands that keep me moving around, crawling around, bending and lifting and struggling with one thing or another.

Regards,
Hammond

October 23, 2014 Tiring Retirement

We have a big production of fish, crabs, shrimp, pears, pecans, okra, greens, tomatoes, eggplant, lemons, grapefruit, oranges, guavas, figs, asparagus, beets, turnips, peppers, pomegranates, making demands. Crabs come from traps right off our dock. Sandra is determined to utilize all this stuff even if it wears her out. Like, what do you do with a bunch of pomegranates? This morning she was wanting to make dyes from some of these things. I hope she does not go out and buy a sheep to get something to die. If so, spinning wheel comes next, then loom and so on. we seem to be going backward in time in some respects, and just don't have time for it all, being retired and all. This retired thing is wearing us out.

2015

July 31, 2015 Judicial Workload

Here in New Orleans a black woman named Crinel has been indicted for Medicare fraud.

Judge number one who is a woman issued a warrant for Crinels arrest. Crinel claimed the warrant was invalid because it was just racial bias. Judge number two ruled that the warrant was valid even though the husband of Judge number one was both Crinels lawyer and lover.
We need more facts to fully evaluate this situation.

August 28, 2015 Making Furniture

Dear Friends

What have you been doing? You ask. Could be rhetorical, or not. Anyway, a short answer does not suffice and long answer is an imposition, so, stop whenever you want and I won't ever know.

One thing is occasionally making furniture. Latest bedside cabinet photos are attached. This took about a week to make, starting with rough cut walnut boards about an inch thick.

These boards have a longer and more interesting history and hardship than some people. Logged in TN by my college roommate Guy Thurmond about 30 years ago, kiln dried pre Katrina, about a ton of them hauled here by pickup, stacked downstairs, flooded and mudded by Katrina, hauled back to TN, kiln dried again, hauled back here, flooded at least once more, maybe twice, in the Ivan, Gustav, Georges timeframe, hauled up into our attic, dried again by high attic heat for at least 5 years, then brought down, culled, planed, resawed, to make something.

One thing i have been having fun doing is making secret compartments. This cabinet has one, with a volume of about one cubic foot. No one would ever suspect such a thing. Casually looking inside and out and opening cabinet doors and the drawer, you will not find it. For, it appears that there is no possible place for it. But, if you knew to look for it, i am sure you would discover it. Some other secret compartments in other structures, I could tell you were there, and you most likely would never find them. One such compartment is in my shop. A friend with DEA was here, used to looking for drugs. I told him there was such a compartment, kinda large, go find it. He failed. This is an example of trickery and illusion to be later explained.

Centuries ago, when hand crafted desks, large and beautiful, were being made and used, they frequently had secret compartments for storing documents. If you make the whole thing, there is a grand opportunity to make document compartments in places where the thickness of the structure cannot be discerned. For instance, just looking at a wall, you cannot tell how thick it is. Go to the other side, you still cannot tell how thick it is.

In the DEA example, downstairs, some of the studs are exposed, walled over completely on one side, partially on the other side. On the partially walled side, which was partially walled with plywood, I took a matching piece of plywood about 4 ft high, 3 ft wide, painted it white like the other parts of the wall, and attached it with hidden hinges on one side and a hidden sliding bolt lock on the other side. If you knew where the bolt locks were, what they were, and how they operated, you could work your hand around various obstructions and touch the right spot and rotate it and slide it and one side of panel would swing out.

The illusion part here is a key diversion. All these panels are nailed rather crudely to the studs, so you can see the nail heads. I took a bunch of nails and cut them off to the thickness of the plywood, and hammered them into the plywood along the line of the studs, just like the other panels that were nailed on. The inspector, seeing panels nailed on, does not consider that they are fake nails. I do realize that in a real search, just like the cops used to find the hidden ransom money in the attic of the guy who kidnapped Lindbergh's kid, that things can be torn apart and anything hidden discovered, or as, (Eldon) the border patrol disassembles some vehicles.

Another fine method is available where a hallway has dark cheap wainscoting that has fake seams that consist of small routed out grooves to simulate different boards. This wainscoting has trim above and below the cheap paneling, which is typically in the range of 3 feet high. One can take a razor knife and jam it in the grooves and cut it top to bottom with a cut so thin it becomes invisible. Then, go several grooves over and do it again, and you have a removable panel. Cut the top off some so this panel can be slipped up under the upper trim and dropped behind the lower trim, and you have the hidden compartment. Drill a tiny hole in the center of this panel, in one of the groves. Then get a nail that fits this hole as a sort of key. To get at the secret compartment, put the nail just in the hole and lift, and up comes the panel, tilt the bottom out, and remove it.

I have a table here that has two secret compartments that would be a challenge for anyone to discover and open. Who knows what will be in these compartments 100 years from now. Maybe all the money and gold i put in there and then died without telling anyone.

Blessings,
Hammond

October 26, 2015 Yippee

Streets are flooded. dock way underwater, water lapping the back steps, in the yard to the citrus trees, covering the front sidewalks, up in the driveway to the truck. We don't have to go to school today.

Uh oh. 65 year time warp. Not in grammar school anymore. Childhood a dim memory over the horizon. No running in the water with my shoes on. No playing in the rain. No sopping wet clothes to mess up the house. No making mud pies or toy boats. Sob. Sob. Try to be an adult. Eat and drink our way through this crisis. Struggle by with 3 freezers of food and a very spiritual and copious cabinet of beverages.

Contributions can be made by credit or debit card to my website.

2016 - 2018

March 1, 2016 Castration

Reaching up overhead to cut loose the hanging clusters of grapefruit reminds me of the time Paul Bunyan asked me to castrate Babe the blue ox.

I thought i should try my hand at poetry
Army spaghetti
Should be the size of a pencil lead
Is the size of the pencil instead.
(what do you think?)
No? Oh well.

Bob observed that he is not observant
Dan told me that submarines could go up the Mississippi to New Orleans
Mike Glad gave me 2000 songs.

May 1, 2017 Ichabod and the Snake

A great egret (white, big) has taken up residence much of the time on our lower patio. His name is Ichabod. When we are down there, he walks between the chairs wanting a handout, like a dog. He will get on the table looking at our food, deciding what to grab. Sandra has explained stuff to him but he goes unheeding to manners. When we are not there but the shop is open, he walks around the shop or just parks there, waiting.

Casting the net from the dock, he stands in the way watching the net come in waiting for food, which he attacks like a bullet fired from a gun. Shrimp and fish.

Early in the season, like late winter, fresh water catfish come in. They are the best eating fish, that is, we are doing the eating, in these waters. So, i set some trot lines, strung between our dock and the one next door, string of hooks baited with chicken gizzards. Gizzards are tough enough to stay on the hook for a while. Two weeks of this and no catfish. But a nice one got in the crab trap, which reminded me, upon eating the fried fillets, of how good they were.

While this is going on, the martin houses are rife with martins, dozens zooming around in the air, in and out of the apartments in the colonial bird house, of which we have two atop poles. Lower down, we have some duck boxes for whistling ducks which are here in abundance, going in and out the duck box, hanging out in Lake Murano, which is the perpetually flooded cul de sac at the end of our street, a few feet from our driveway. Occasionally a duck lands on the martin house and causes all sorts of dive bombing and raucous protests from the martins.

So, having a failed trot line experience, and pile of chicken gizzards left over, and Ichabod walking under foot to the extent of being a hazard, i decided to see if he wanted chicken gizzards. Cut them in half, two meaty chunks, which he snatched up with relish, eating them like grapes, a bottomless pit, as it goes.

Every now and then Ich goes on alert, points like a bird dog, head stone still, body stone still, neck vibrating left to right, about a quarter inch movement, staring intently where his nose is pointing. He started doing this, aiming out into the yard. Nothing to be seen by human senses out there. But he dashed forward into the grassy yard, stopped and pointed again, dashed forward again and struck, pulling up a two-foot snake, garter or ribbon. Struggle started, Ich chomping left and right trying to quell the coiling and struggling the snake was doing.

Ich would quickly open his bill, jerk to one side and regrip the snake and chomp some more. In this process, the snake got away, racing for the dock and cover, Ich hot on his heels, like a tiny version of a dinosaur attack. He got the snake just short of the dock. Chomping started again, Ich trying to get to the head.

Ich eventually succeeded, chomping the head over and over and trying to get it started down his throat. Egret has short comb like projections along the edges of his bill, serving as small gripping teeth. By and by he got the head going down, and it was a long struggle getting more snake in, but inch by inch he was succeeding. Finally, it reached the point where all the snake save about 10 inches was down the throat.

The last of the snake started wrapping around the egret bill, at the tip, where Ich could not open his bill to get the snake further in. This continued as a stalemate for a while, Ich trying to chomp, snake tail whipping round and round the bill trying to stop the progress. Eventually bit by bit the snake was taken in and gone. Ich came back to the patio and stood around in a stupor for a while, neck retracted.

Sandra and I ate a bunch of crabs caught off the dock, and had some spirits, as the day waned.

April 4, 2018 Big Al

Strangbean (not his real name), a friend living on the edge of the Atchafalaya swamp in SW LA, is under threat from Big Al, or was. Big Al is an alligator, a dozen feet long by careful estimate or exaggeration of several people.

The swamp is cypress, cypress knees, other trees and vegetation, black freshwater, much of it with floating vegetation. Not navigable in many places. It is loaded with alligators. Big Al is the biggest, and the main threat that worries

Strangbean and his family and his dogs, assuming dogs think about stuff like that when it is not immediately in front of their nose.

The swamp is on two sides of Strangbean's house, closest point about the distance a big alligator can strike from. Big Al roams around as evidenced by various sighting and tracks across the road. Neighborhood dogs are disappearing. Strangbean and his wife Millie have small children, a couple of dogs and two rabbits. The whole menagerie plays in the yard, creating much too much anxiety on the parent's part. They tried to get Big Al trapped, but that has not worked out.

From Strangbean's yard, there is a narrow opening in the vegetation, that has been narrowing as spring proceeds, through which, off in the distance in the swamp, an old fallen tree has resulted in a log just above water, at an angle. From a very specific position in his yard, with binoculars, one can see this log, and see that Big Al likes to sun on it at times. As of this writing, he is not feeding just yet, that will come as the season progresses. So, occasionally one or more small alligators are walking around on his back. Later this year, those smaller alligators will no long be among the living, they will be among the fed on, fed on by Big Al.

Strangbean showed me this situation, and explained that he and his family were worried constantly about the danger and he had no solution but the trapper who had done nothing. From the yard, Big Al, when on the log, was way the health out in the swamp. But even at that distance, and even with the vegetative cover intervening, he was so skittish that a slight movement by us in Strangbean's yard caused Al to slide into the water. With the wind blowing there was one bush that moved into the sight line to Big Al at times during which he was just plain out of sight.

This was worrisome, to the extent that I dreamed about it that night. Specifically, in the dream, I told Millie I would shoot the gator from her yard if she wished. Both Strangbean and Millie and the kids wanted this done and

228

settled, so we agreed that Strangbean would try to find a pattern to Big Al's sunning himself and we would go from there.

Checking the weather, it appeared that the Wednesday after Easter might be good, so i told him i would come out then. I intended to set up a table with sand bags and sit there from 2pm on.

I got there on time and Big Al was in position, on the log, facing away at about a 45-degree angle. I started moving very slowly, in the shadows, to get my equipment in position, looking at Big Al at times, and at where i was going at times. Big Al slipped away even so. Got my stuff ready and sat there with binoculars for 2 hours before anything happened. What happened was a small alligator crawled out on the log and parked. Watch resumed.

I wanted to see Big Al crawl out on the log to see just how he got up there, and had been carefully watching mostly continuously, for this reason, as well as being prepared for the big event. Looked down for a moment and like magic he was there. Did not see how he got there.

But, there was a stump at one end, and he was mostly behind that stump. Stump covered him from about the pelvis forward. One hind leg visible, nothing accessible to a bullet forward of the hind leg. In the position on the log partly behind the stump, I dreamed of shooting him through the pelvis, with handloaded 120 grain bullet going up toward 3500 feet per second, which would involve shooting through the stem of a bush that appeared to be about a foot toward me from Big Al. I thought this would probably do the trick but was a last resort.

I got up and eased over about 20 feet to the side to see if there were some opening in the bushes that would let me shoot from another position and get in a better shot. Nothing doing with that, could not even see the gator. Eased back to the table, got the binoculars and could hardly believe my eyes. Big Al had turned completely around and all except his enormous tail was now visible. Knowing how spooky this guy was I was thinking he was going to slide out of sight any second.

He was about 45 degrees off broadside, facing away from me, on the log, tilted up toward his head at about 20 degrees. I figured if i shot him in center of the last left rib the bullet would take out everything in his thoracic cavity and there would be no doubt as to the outcome. Squeezed it off.

Dreamed that he was knocked sideways, big spray of blood at entry point, blood running down the log, gator completely immobile, hanging precariously off the log on the other side. I expected a lot of thrashing around etc, but nothing. Dead, not a twitch. Left front foot, webbed, stuck stiffly out to the side, foot spread, frozen in place. Like he got completely paralyzed in this position. Stayed just like this for several minutes, then slowly slid over the other side of the log as gravity pulled the heavy front end and belly into the water. Not recoverable.

I saw Strangbean in the bar he frequents on the bayou by his house a couple of weeks later. He said for me to forget about Big Al as Al had not been seen recently and must have gone somewhere else. He asked me why the law was so picky about just shooting these big dangerous gators that were around populated areas, wanting to trap and transplant them instead. Don't we have enough big gators without doing that, he said. Cops routinely shoot dangerous dogs. Even shot a yellow lab for growling at them. What's with this gator nonsense, he asked. Even Tucker Carlson had a program on it, kill the big gators, don't mess around with it, they eat people and pets. I told him it is all politically correct nonsense, hyped by liberal dilettantes. We haven't had a gator shortage in ages. It makes about as much sense as the Jefferson parish cops trying to trap and relocate nutrias that plague the city canals instead of shooting them as they do. Shoot a pest nutria, shoot a dangerous gator, what's the difference?

April 4, 2018 Potato Mortality

People have harmless fun throughout the land with a homemade PVC pipe contraption that shoots a potato up into the air. Jefferson parish, right next to the famous Orleans, parish thusly made the news:

Two knuckleheads, as the sheriff later described them, saw a YouTube video about how to make this thing, got the parts, made it, fired it off behind the high board fence in their backyard. Neighbor called the police and reported gunfire.

Police came, went up to the high board gate that led to the back yard, opened the gate, got growled at by the dog in the backyard, drew their gun. Knuckleheads yelled not to shoot the dog. The cop shot and killed the dog.

This was determined to be what is described as a righteous shooting, or a good shooting.

What is the moral of this event? I just don't know. Maybe it's that time is so short, or situations so crazy, or people are so scared, or cops are so jumpy, that the outcomes are crazy.

TP (Times Picayune) missed their chance. Dog killing linked to potato gun.

August 14, 2018 Exquisite Choreography in 5 Seconds

Heading south on I-65 approaching Gulf coast. Road wet from recent rain. Three lanes of traffic filled with vehicles. Far left was concrete jersey barriers at outer edge of paved shoulder, then paved shoulder, then three lanes of traffic, then the shoulder on the right side. We were in the left most traffic lane. To our left was the paved shoulder, then left of that the concrete barriers. No vehicles immediately ahead of us. In lane to our right, the center lane, up ahead, was a tractor trailer. Just behind, center lane, was a small red sports car convertible, top down, packed with an adult and kids, hair blowing in the wind. In far-right lane, a stream of traffic, containing a jeep station wagon

SUV, Cherokee, somewhat ahead of us. All traffic going somewhere around 65 mph.

Suddenly the SUV jeep in the far-right lane rotated 90 degrees to the left, went sliding sideways at 65 mph and progressing across all lanes, passing immediately behind the tractor trailer, progressing across the path of the little red car, and directly into our path. I hit the brakes, Ford F150 crew cab, antilock started jerking and releasing, truck stayed perfectly straight, headed for impact into the side of jeep. Then it appeared that it was possible that we might clear it by inches as we jerked to slower speeds, but that would not happen because it was headed nose first for the concrete barrier, which would stop it with half of the SUV still in our lane. Braced for impact. Immediately before impact, the SUV rotated again 90 degrees to the left and came up against the concrete barrier on its right side, facing oncoming traffic, but moving out of our path like a gate opening. We missed contact by a microsecond and inches. We were not hit from behind. This entire episode, start to finish, Sandra and I estimated occurred in 5 seconds. About a half minute after this started, the traffic mass was just as it was before the incident, as if it never happened. We are not aware of any reaction the little red car took, back beside us, hair blowing in the wind.

The SUV impact with the concrete appeared minimal from the brief glimpse i had of it. I don't think anyone got hurt in any vehicle.

IN THE BELLY OF THE SNAKE

Pastor John in his little garden
Thanks to Elva's diligence
Watches the wrens, and the baby wrens
Feeding and getting fed
And the blue birds and the baby blue birds
Feeding and getting fed
And it is so idyllic
A deceptive peacefulness
Hammond and Sandy had the blue bird house
The 4 baby blue birds getting fed daily
Watched daily
One morning, where were they? gone
In the bird house, a 5 foot rat snake
With 4 lumps strung out in its body
H knows this is the food chain
Nevertheless, he chops the snake in parts
And takes out the baby birds, too late.
But satisfying somehow, trying to undo.
Not far away
Lurks the apex predator
A seven hundred pound alligator
Swallowing creatures whole in the dark of night
And we must know
The apex predators are all around us

Some slither, some fly, some walk
On 4 legs, lots of them on 2 legs
And the effect of the 2-legged apex predators
Is often on us without our realizing it is happening
Till we wake up and discover that the innocents
Are in the belly of the snake.

AUTUMN BY THE SEA

Water lapping at the dock
bare now, released of its grand purpose
berth for stately sailing vessel
Armordillo, absent now

Sun rise.......corals, pinks, lavenders
Dressing morning in her splendid garb
Water......curving out of sight
Like paths unknown, ...yet beckoning
Her siren call,.....distant now.....

Pelicans......winging slowly
on deliberate course
Marsh hens announcing
Breaking day

Martin houses
Silent......empty.......like the rooms
Inside.........no children
Clattering, clamoring, in that last minute rush
for the school bus

Two of us reside.,...and yet,
memories full and sweet resound
of family and rowdy, handsome boys
filled with joy of living

and quickened minds

Thoughts abound in thankful praise to GOD
For Life, for Love and bounty of this breaking day
For Life, for Love and bounty of this breaking day

Sandra A Eve, September 21,2011

The End